Collins

LITTLE BOOKS

CW00958439

SCRABBLE®

BRAND Crossword Game

SECRETS

HarperCollins Publishers
Westerhill Road
Bishopbriggs
Glasgow
G64 2QT

HarperCollins Publishers
1st Floor, Watermarque Building
Ringsend Road, Dublin 4, Ireland

Fourth edition 2020

10 9 8 7 6 5 4 3 2 1

© HarperCollins Publishers 2011, 2014, 2016, 2018, 2020

ISBN 978-0-00-839583-4

www.collinsdictionary.com
www.harpercollins.co.uk/scrabble

A catalogue record for this book is available from the British Library

Typeset by Davidson Publishing Solutions, Glasgow

Printed and bound in the UK by Pureprint

If you would like to comment on any aspect of this book, please contact us at the above address or online.
E-mail: puzzles@harpercollins.co.uk
facebook.com/collinsdictionary
@collinsdict

Written by: Mark Nyman

Contents

Foreword

Mark Nyman is the antithesis of a Scrabble geek! He is a man from the real world who happens to be one of the greatest Scrabble players of all time. In this gem of a book utilising a mixture of mischievousness, wit and masterful expertise he is able to showcase the game as interesting, enjoyable and enormous fun.

I met Mark in 1992 when awestruck by his word game abilities in an international tournament in Bangkok. I will always remember his kindness in addressing my newbie questions at length. He helped to inspire me to devote myself to learning the game and just two years later we faced each other in a professional game in the USA. He won!

Though aimed at the beginner, there is something for everyone in this updated edition of *Scrabble Secrets* from what to do with too many vowels, and what prefixes and suffixes to look for, to pertinent advice about those valuable tiles the 'S' and the blank.

Mark's skill extends well beyond vocabulary and strategy, however, to such subjects as handling winning and losing, maintaining a poker-face, skulduggery and even the question of cheating. We also find out why he hangs around the bathroom in between important games…

Scrabble Secrets and its 100 plus top tips will delight you and hopefully encourage even the most casual player to consider taking the game more seriously by joining a club or entering a competitive tournament.

Gerry Carter
1998 Asia Pacific Scrabble Champion

Gerry Carter is the originator of the Facebook Forum '*Scrabble International*'

1 | Two's Company

Scrabble study always starts with the two-letter words. The most useful of these are the ones with the highest-scoring letters, i.e. the Q and Z. So let's begin with the four most useful words in Scrabble:

QI	Life force
ZA	Pizza
ZE	Gender-neutral pronoun
ZO	Himalayan cattle

So if an I, A, E or O is directly below or to the right of a triple-letter square, you could place the Q or Z on it and, if you can go across/down with the same word, a potential 62 points can be picked up, much to the consternation of your opponent!

A common myth amongst Scrabble beginners is that the longer the word, the higher the score – this is not necessarily true at all.

You may AGONIZE for as little as 17 if you don't make good use of the premium squares, whereas as in secret 1 a simple ZA, ZE or ZO might get you 62 on the same turn – be economical with your tiles.

S, C and P respectively are the most common starting letters and together comprise over a quarter of the words in the dictionary. So when moving your rack around it's a good idea to put them at the beginning – a profusion of words arise from such useful prefixes as:

SEMI-, SUB-
CH-, CO-
POLY-, PRE-

Meaning-less?

Whether or not to insist on knowing the meanings of words played is a controversial topic and can lead to lots of arguments.

The official rule is that you don't have to know them, but some people still think it's just not right. If you are playing at home and insist on knowing the meanings it can lead to trouble because it's a moot point how close you have to get to the exact definition. For example, you may play ZLOTY knowing it's a type of currency, but your opponent may insist on you explaining from which country it originates. If you don't know, will they let you have the word?

These inconsistencies can cause a fallout, so far better to stick to the 'not having to know' rule for peace's sake. It's great to find out the meanings, but when there are over 160,000 Scrabble words with 9 letters or less, it would take an incredible mind to know every meaning as well as every word.

Personally, I would rather learn a new word than a meaning of an existing word I know (shock horror), but I do enjoy picking up some of the meanings along the way. Former World Champion Pakorn Nemitrmansuk from Thailand struggles with fluent

English and doesn't bother with the meanings of the more outlandish words.

On the other hand, Scrabble is a great learning tool for improving vocabulary, so at the end of the day it's whatever floats your boat. Just don't sneer at your opponent if they don't know a definition unless you think they'd do the same to you.

The six-letter combination PARDON goes with every vowel to make an unusual seven-letter word and thereby give a possible 50-point bonus:

PARDON + A   PANDORA – sea bream
        + E   PADRONE – Italian inn owner
        + I   PONIARD – dagger
        + O   PANDOOR – one of an 18th-century force of Croatian soldiers
        + U   PANDOUR – "   "   "   "

By the way PARDON ME is an anagram of POMANDER and I PARDON ME is an anagram of MEROPIDAN – a bird of the bee-eater family – and PROMENADE ap-piers to be an anagram of PARDON MEE.

6 | No Rush

Use all of your twenty-five minutes when you play to a clock. Don't rush into playing the first move you think of – there's usually a better move you haven't spotted yet.

It's also worth giving yourself a couple of extra seconds after placing your move on the board and before hitting the clock to make sure you're happy with it.

7 | Hello Hello Hello

There are no less than thirteen different variations of the word HELLO:

HALLO
HALLALOO
HALLOA
HALLOO
HILLO
HILLOA
HOLLA
HOLLO
HOLLOA
HOLLOO
HULLO
HULLOA
HULLOO

They are all verbs (apart from HALLALOO) and HALLOES, HELLOES, HILLOES, HOLLOES and HULLOES are also okay, so there are forty-five derivatives altogether.

8 Irritable Vowel Syndrome

Too many vowels on your rack can lead to disaster.
Generally, the ideal ratio of consonants to vowels is 4:3.
So having four vowels is a slight overload but fairly easily
remedied – five or more and the alarm bells start ringing.

In this case, it can take two or three turns to restore
the balance, and the worst of it is you are unlikely to
score well in the meantime since the vowels are worth
only one point at face value.

Here are some examples of lovely **vowelly** words to
get you out of trouble quickly:

AE	one
AI	slow moving shaggy South American animal
EA	a river
IO	moth
OI	shout for attention
OU	man
AIA	Eastern female servant
AUA	mullet
AUE	Māori exclamation
EAU	a river
EUOI	a cry of Bacchic frenzy
EUOUAE	a Gregorian cadence

It's amazing how often EUOI especially comes up –
those followers of Bacchus had some fun didn't they?

A Fine Mess

You can easily get out of a sticky situation with
multiple As if you know some of these:

AA	volcanic lava
AAL	Asian tree
ABA	Syrian camel-haired cloth
AKA	New Zealand vine
ALA	wing
AMA	water vessel
ANA	collection of reminiscences
AVA	Polynesian shrub
AWA	away
CAA	to call
FAA	fall
MAA	to bleat
ACAI	Brazilian berry
ANOA	small cattle
ATUA	demon
AULA	hall
ABACA	Philippine plant
ALAAP	Indian rhythm
ALAPA	" "
ANANA	pineapple
ARABA	Asian carriage
TAATA	father
ARAARA	game fish
TAIAHA	Māori staff

E is the most common letter and the best vowel to hold. You can really struggle with a dearth of Es in the game – they are its lifeblood – but on the flip side, you don't really want more than a couple on your rack at any one time. Because there are twelve in the set, you can quite often find yourself with three or four Es – here are a few words to Es the problem:

EE	eye
EEN	eyes
EEW	expression of disgust
EME	uncle
ENE	even
JEE	to move ahead
MEE	Malaysian noodle dish
EEEW	expression of greater disgust
EEVEN	evening
ELPEE	long-playing record
ETWEE	small case
EXEME	to set free
GELEE	jelly
ENTETE	obsessed
VEEPEE	vice president
VENEWE	venue

Do, however, try and keep one E back on your rack unless the score with it is too good to miss.

It's amazing how regularly you can get stuck with two or three Is on your rack and, if you're not careful, the problem can persist. To dig you out of the I-hole sooner rather than later, try playing the following:

IWI	Māori tribe	AALII	bushy shrub
BIDI	Indian cigarette	BIKIE	motorcycle gang member
DIVI	stupid person		
FINI	finish	CIVIE	civilian
HILI	scar on a seed	DIXIE	cooking pot
IMID	a drug	FIXIT	solution to a problem
INIA	points at the back of the head		
		LITAI	Lithuanian monetary unit
IRID	iris		
IXIA	African plant	MIRIN	Japanese rice wine
LIRI	monetary unit		
NIDI	insects' nests	OIDIA	fungal spores
PILI	Philippine tree	TEIID	lizard
TITI	South American monkey	VISIE	to look
		YITIE	bunting
WILI	spirit	ZIMBI	cowrie shell

12 | O My Word

A surfeit of Os is relatively easy to alleviate, but here's a soupçon of gems to make it even simpler:

OO	wool
OBO	ship carrying oil
ONO	Hawaiian fish
OOM	old man's title of respect
OOR	our
OOT	out
OXO	acid containing oxygen
OLIO	dish of differing ingredients
ORZO	pasta
OVOLO	convex moulding
GOOROO	guru
HOOROO	hurrah

The U is by far the least useful of the vowels, unless of course accompanied by the Q. More than one U can really cramp your style and flow, but there are a few unusual multiple U-words that can help:

ULU	knife
UMU	oven
UTU	reward
BUBU	African garment
HUHU	hairy New Zealand beetle
KURU	nervous disease
LULU	outstanding person
PUPU	Hawaiian dish
RURU	owl
SULU	Fijian sarong
UNAU	two-toed sloth
URUS	extinct European ox
YUZU	citrus fruit
AHURU	Pacific cod
BUTUT	Gambian monetary unit
DURUM	Mediterranean wheat
QUIPU	Incan recording device
UHURU	national independence
URUBU	bird
MUUMUU	Hawaiian dress

A player's vocabulary is their ammunition in the game. It's not the 'be all and end all' but the more words you know, the more you should improve. An average person's vocabulary is between 10–15,000 words, i.e. about 10% of all the words useful to Scrabble, so there's plenty of scope for improvement.

Don't be put off at the thought of having to learn 100,000 new words. If you're willing to give it a go, you can be economical with your study as some words are a lot more 'Scrabble-friendly' than others. The best players probably know about half of them and there are only a handful of people close to knowing the lot – and they definitely need to get out more...

15 | Size Matters

The two-letter words are the bread and butter of Scrabble, and learning them is by no means an insurmountable task. There are just 127 twos of which about a third are everyday words anyway, so learning two or three a day will crack them all in the space of a month.

Next come the 1340 three-letter words. Only the top players know all these, but it's surprising how many you will pick up with practice.

The more weird and wonderful 4s and 5s are reserved for the serious player – if you're starting out on the competitive road, it's best to kick off by learning those with the high-scoring letters.

The 6s aren't as important as you might think and probably come last in a study regime. However, there are some fabulous six-letter blockers worth knowing.

The high-probability 7s and 8s are really useful in the search for that treasured 50-point bonus. There are about 34,000 seven-letter words in all and 42,000 eights, but don't let that deter you. Knowledge of the most likely 250 of each will improve your game immensely.

Nine-letter (or longer) words come up very rarely, though it's incredibly satisfying when they do. In terms of Scrabble study don't worry about them – that saves you looking at half the dictionary.

16 Some Real Corkers

Here's an A to Z of some of my favourite 7s and 8s:

AZULEJO	Spanish porcelain tile
BUHUNDS	Norwegian dogs
CONEPATL	skunk
DWEEBISH	quite stupid
EUPHRASY	annual plant
FIREFANG	to overheat through decomposition
GUNKHOLE	to go on short boat excursions
HEITIKI	Māori neck ornament
ICEKHANA	motor race on frozen lake
JEREPIGO	fortified wine
KERCHOO	atishoo
LUNKHEAD	stupid person
MRIDANGA	Indian drum
NUDZHES	nudges
OLYCOOK	American doughnut
PATOOTIE	person's bottom
QUETZAL	Central American bird
RUDESBY	rude person
SLYBOOTS	sly person
TAGHAIRM	divination sought by lying in a bullock's hide under a Scottish waterfall

UNSHRUBD	not having shrubs
VEEJAYS	video jockeys
WOSBIRD	illegitimate child
XERAFIN	Indian coin
YAHOOISM	crudeness
ZEDOARY	Asian stem used as a stimulant

17 | Time for a Change

There is a great deal of skill in choosing the right time to change your letters, as well as which ones to throw back in the bag.

The first, and most important, tip on this subject is DON'T BE AFRAID TO CHANGE. You may score zero on that particular turn, but if the alternative is to be left with a horrible combination of letters, like IIIUVVW, you may get stuck scoring 10 points per move for several turns. Say you average 20 points per turn, it's better to change and score a likely 60 over the next three moves than 40 without the change.

The most 50-point bonus-conducive letters are
AEINRST – generally, when throwing tiles in the bag,
you want to keep one of any of these that you hold on
your rack, as long as you leave a decent consonant to
vowel ratio (i.e. 3:2, 2:2, 2:1, 1:1). The highest scoring
letters JQXZ are only worth keeping if there are some
tasty triple-letter and triple-word squares available
to play onto the board. If the board is tight and
especially if there are no floating vowels, the high-
scorers could be rendered useless. The X and Z are
generally more fruitful than the J and Q if you can't
resist holding one back.

In my opinion, the converse of AEINRST is FGJQUVW – i.e. these are the seven worst letters in the set. So, when changing, always get rid of these unless you have the Q with a U, a high-scoring place for the J, or a promising -ING combination. Even then you might be held back, especially if the board is tight.

You may be surprised about the inclusion of the G, but in my experience Gs are generally bad news. If you're deciding to change, always throw back a V if you have one. V is the weakest letter of all, partly because it's the only one that doesn't form a two-letter word. As for the rest – BCDHKLMOPXYZ – they all have their merits and it depends on the state of the board as to whether any of them are worth keeping. Usually chuck them though.

MAX- is a handy prefix and produces some lovely extensions:

MAXED	reached full extent
MAXI	large racing yacht
MAXICOAT	long coat
MAXILLA	upper jawbone
MAXIMIN	highest of set of minimum values
MAXIMITE	explosive
MAXIMUS	method rung on twelve bells
MAXING	reaching full extent
MAXIXE	Brazilian dance
MAXWELL	unit of magnetic flux

There's also SUPERMAX – relating to the very highest levels of security.

Here's a selection of words to a-stone-ish you:

ASTONE	astonish
BURSTONE	hard rock
CAMSTONE	limestone
EARSTONE	calcium carbonate crystal in the ear
HISTONE	DNA protein
ICESTONE	cryolite
LAPSTONE	cobbler's device
POTSTONE	used for making cooking vessels
ROESTONE	limestone
RUBSTONE	used for sharpening
STONERAG	lichen
STONERAW	"
SUNSTONE	feldspar
TINSTONE	black or brown stone

There's also the nine-letter IRONSTONE, which is a very nice anagram of SEROTONIN, and LIMESTONE and MILESTONE are both anagrams of LEMONIEST and MELONIEST.

Take the Rough with the Smooth

Certain mini-combinations of consonants work really well together and are worth holding on to in the search for a 50-point bonus. They often tend to comprise both 'hard' and 'soft' letters but it's best not to keep back all 'hard' letters together and likewise all 'soft'.

'Hard' consonants   BDFGJKPQTVX

'Soft' consonants   HLMNRSWYZ

I've left out C as it can be both 'soft' and 'hard' – this adaptability is why it's a particular favourite.

So..........

Consonant combinations particularly worth keeping back for potential bonus play:

BL, BM, BR, CH, CK, CL, CN, CP, CR, CT, DL, DN, DR, HP, KL, KN, KR, LP, MP, NT, PR, RT

BDR, BLR, BMR, CDR, CHN, CHR, CHT, CLR, CLT, CNR, CNT, CPR, CRT, DLR, DNR, DPR, DRT, GLN, GNR, HPR, HPT, KLN, KLR, KNR, KNT, LPR, LPT, MPR, NRT, PRT

An S is always worth holding on to in addition to these combinations. You will see they all contain at least one 'hard' and one 'soft' letter.

Consonant combinations to avoid (using 3-point or lower tiles):

BG, BP, CG, DT, GP, GT, LN

BDT, BGP, BGT, BPT, DGP, DGT, GPT, LNR

You will notice that all these contain either all 'soft' or all 'hard' letters. Of course, any combination with two of the same letter and you automatically look to offload the duplicate.

It can be good anagram practice to look at car number plates and try to find the shortest word you can using all the letters within them. Add any extra letters you want but the less the better, for example:

SKO5 CYJ   JOCKEYS (beats JOYSTICK)

NCL2 END   INCLINED (beats DECLINING)

OWO6 ETA   TEAKWOOD (beats TAEKWONDO)

This can be great fun and very satisfying on a long car journey but don't forget to concentrate on the road as well. Of course, you won't be able to find a word with all the plates – if you see QXO7 GJZ, give up immediately and move on to the next car.

26 Tasty Twosomes

There are some gorgeous seven- and eight-letter anagram pairs – here are some of my favourites:

APPRIZE	ZAPPIER
BOGEYMAN	MONEYBAG
CRUMPETS	SPECTRUM
DOORBELL	BORDELLO
ELATION	TOENAIL
FLUSHING	LUNGFISH (freshwater fish)
GHETTOED	DOGTEETH (carved ornaments)
HOGMANAY	MAHOGANY
IFFIEST	FIFTIES
JITTERS	TRIJETS (jets with three engines)
KIDNAPS	SKIDPAN (slippery area)
LIMEADE	EMAILED
MOORHEN	HORMONE
NAPPIES	PINESAP (red herb)
OOMPAHS	SHAMPOO
PRESUME	SUPREME
QUERIES	ESQUIRE
RINGTONE	NITROGEN
SCREWTOP	CROWSTEP (set of steps to the top of a gable)

TAPEWORM	POMWATER (kind of apple)
UTOPIAN	OPUNTIA (cactus)
VIOLATED	DOVETAIL
WASPNEST	STEWPANS
XEROTIC	EXCITOR (nerve)
YACKERS	SCREAKY
ZINCITE	CITIZEN

XEROTIC is not as kinky as it sounds – it relates to dryness of bodily tissues.

As a general rule, all US alternative spellings are allowed in Scrabble, so color, humor, neighbor, etc. are OK – like it or not. Also, almost every -ISE verb can be spelt with -IZE. It's interesting that Collins is recognised everywhere in the World as the English Scrabble 'bible', apart from the US and Canada, where they use Webster's. Since Collins incorporates all of Webster's and a lot more, you ironically need to unlearn loads of words to play in the States. This seems a reflection of the US 'we are the world' attitude, so don't bother playing serious Scrabble over there.

South America is a relatively unexplored continent dictionary-wise – there's plenty of scope for future great words from that neck of the woods.

'I'm a Believer' in monkeys – they keep ape-earing in the official Scrabble word list:

BANDARI	MICO
CEBID	OUAKARI
COAITA	OUISTITI
DOUC	SAGOUIN
ENTELLUS	SAIMIRI
GRIVET	SAJOU
GUEREZA	TALAPOIN
HANUMAN	TAMARIN
JOCKO	VERVET
LANGUR	WANDEROO
MANGABEY	ZATI

The beautiful CYNOMOLGI have to be worth a mention, however unlikely they are to jump out at you.

Slang words are perfectly allowable in Scrabble when they become common English usage. A lot of Australian slang appears, such as:

ALF	an uncultivated Australian
SIK	excellent
ACCA	an academic
ALKO	alcoholic
DACK	to forcefully remove trousers
DOCO	documentary
DORB	stupid person
DRAC	unattractive
GOOG	egg
KERO	kerosene
KYBO	temporary camping lavatory
MYXO	myxomatosis
NOAH	shark
UMPY	umpire
WARB	insignificant person
FIRIE	firefighter
NIXER	spare-time job
UMPIE	umpire

SLANGUAGE is a word in itself – a lovely front hook to 'language'.

There are plenty of exotic -BIRD words to fly by you:

AXEBIRD	nightjar
BOOBIRD	person who boos
COWBIRD	American songbird
FATBIRD	nocturnal bird
GAOLBIRD	person confined to jail
HANGBIRD	bird that builds a hanging nest
JAYBIRD	jay
KINGBIRD	American flycatcher
LYREBIRD	Australian bird that spreads its tail into shape of a lyre
MAYBIRD	American songbird
OVENBIRD	small South American bird
PUFFBIRD	tropical American bird
RICEBIRD	bird frequenting rice fields
SNOWBIRD	bird of Arctic regions
WHIPBIRD	whistling bird
YARDBIRD	inexperienced soldier

31 | Abbreviations and Acronyms

Abbreviations are not allowed in themselves unless they come into common conversation, in which case they become colloquialisms, for example AD for advertisement. The same applies to acronyms – there are a few crackers:

ASPRO	associate professor
BAMBI	born-again middle-aged biker
ELINT	electronic intelligence
FEDEX	federal express
JATO	jet-assisted take-off
MIPS	million instructions per second
NOX	nitrogen oxide
POMO	post-modernism
QUANGO	quasi-autonomous non-governmental organisation
RONZER	someone from rest of New Zealand – not Auckland
TASER	Thomas A. Swift's electric rifle
TWOCCING	taking without owner's consent
WAAC	member of Women's Auxiliary Arms Corps
WOOPIE	well-off older person
YABA	yet another bloody acronym!

The blank is without doubt the best tile in the Scrabble set. If you're lucky enough to get both during the course of the game it will increase your chances of winning hugely, but you need to make the most of them.

If you get a blank early on, try and save it until you can use it in a 50-point bonus word. Never waste it on a move scoring less than 30 points.

Some players get really stuck when a blank appears – it's not surprising when you consider there are effectively twenty-six combinations to think about. But try to envisage the blank as a particular letter on your rack – some are more likely to go well with your other six letters than others. Even so, moves with a blank tend to require a great deal more thought and it's understandable they take longer.

As a general rule, use the blank when your move scores over 20 points more than one without it. Otherwise, hold on for a big play later – it's worth the wait.

Two blanks together can be a real mind-blower as there are 676 potential combinations. Don't panic: the more you play, the more you'll get a feel for which letters you're looking for them to be.

33 | Bonus Play

If you can play out all your letters for the 50-point bonus, you'll enhance your winning chances enormously. Achieving this once in a game is good, twice excellent and three or more times will almost guarantee you victory.

The art of bonus finding is innate to Scrabble success – much of it is to do with rack-balancing along with knowing some high-probability seven- and eight-letter words (i.e. those with the most common letters) to help find that killer move.

There are some great six- and seven-letter combinations to work towards to give yourself the best opportunity of making it happen.

34 Another Retsina

As well as having ten anagrams (you don't need to know them all), RETSINA goes with more letters to make an eight-letter word than any other – so look for these floaters on the board:

A ARTESIAN (well)

B BANISTER

C CANISTER

D STRAINED

E TRAINEES

F FENITARS
   (European plants)

G ANGRIEST

H HAIRNETS

I RAINIEST

J NARTJIES
   (tangerines)

K NARKIEST

L ENTRAILS

M MINARETS

N TRANNIES

O NOTARIES

P PAINTERS

R TRAINERS

S STAINERS

T NITRATES

U URINATES

W TINWARES
   (objects made of
   tin plate)

The six-letter combination ANTIES goes with more letters to make a seven-letter word than any other:

A **ENTASIA** (convex curve)

B **BASINET** (medieval helmet)

C **CINEAST** (film enthusiast)

D **DETAINS**

E **ETESIAN** (Mediterranean wind)

F **FAINEST** (most eager)

G **SEATING**

H **SHEITAN** (Muslim demon)

I **ISATINE** (yellowish-red compound)

J **JANTIES** (petty officers)

K **INTAKES**

L **ENTAILS**

M **INMATES**

N **INANEST**

O **ATONIES** (lack of muscle tone)

P **PANTIES**

R **RETSINA**

S **NASTIES**

T **INSTATE**

U **AUNTIES**

V **NATIVES**

W **TAWNIES**

X **SEXTAIN** (Italian verse)

Z **ZANIEST**

So only Q and Y don't work. Note that there are several anagrams in some cases but knowing one is often enough.

Along with RETSINA, SEATING is the most prolific seven-letter word when it comes to anagrams – it has ten:

EASTING	distance eastwards
EATINGS	
GAINEST	straightest
GENISTA	member of broom family
INGATES	entrances
INGESTA	nourishment
TAGINES	African cooking pots
TANGIES	Orkney water spirits
TEASING	
TSIGANE	Gypsy music

-MAN is a very productive suffix – here are some 7s and 8s you might not expect:

ADWOMAN	woman working in advertising
BRIDEMAN	bridegroom's attendant
CHOREMAN	handyman
DRAGOMAN	Middle Eastern guide
EARTHMAN	inhabitant of the earth
FACEMAN	miner working at coalface
GLEEMAN	minstrel
HELIMAN	helicopter pilot
IRONMAN	very strong man
JURYMAN	member of a jury
KEELMAN	bargeman
LOCOMAN	railwayman
MOTORMAN	driver of electric train
OVERSMAN	overseer
PRIZEMAN	winner of prize
QUILLMAN	clerk
RADIOMAN	radio operator
SWEETMAN	man kept by a woman
TOYWOMAN	woman who sells toys
UNWOMAN	to remove womanly qualities from
VERSEMAN	man who writes verse
WATERMAN	skilled boatman
YEGGMAN	burglar

Part of the attraction of Scrabble is it helps you forget about your worries while you're concentrating on the game. Here are a few suggestions to make it an even more relaxing and positive experience:

(a) Sleep well the night before – a couple of beers or glasses of wine should do the trick

(b) Drink caffeine to stimulate your brain – not too much though as it might get a bit wayward

(c) Drink water – again in moderation as needing the loo will make you lose concentration

(d) Have a massage

(e) Play uplifting music – I find listening to lyrics and being silent (anagram of listen) much more productive than being loud and talking. Put together playlists with your favourite songs and get your earphones on before a game to get you in the right mood.

(f) Avoid stressful work and particularly bad bosses

(g) Avoid affairs

(h) Play in pleasant uncluttered surroundings

(i) Laugh at your opponent if they are over-competitive

(j) Support a winning football team, i.e. Barcelona or QPR

Wood You Believe It?

WOOD works really well as a prefix and suffix:

AGALWOOD	Asian tree
BEARWOOD	bark used as a laxative
CAMWOOD	West African tree
DAGWOOD	European shrub
ELMWOOD	wood from elm tree
FATWOOD	kindling
GUMWOOD	gumtree
HAREWOOD	sycamore
INKWOOD	tree
KINGWOOD	wood of Brazilian leguminous tree
LATEWOOD	formed later in tree's growing season
MILKWOOD	tree producing latex
NUTWOOD	walnut
OVENWOOD	word for burning in oven
PEARWOOD	wood from pear tree
SAPWOOD	soft wood beneath bark
WILDWOOD	forest growing in natural uncultivated state
WOODBIN	box for firewood
WOODFREE	paper from treated pulp
WOODHEN	flightless bird
WOODLORE	woodcraft skills

WOODMEAL	sawdust powder
WOODMICE	field mice
WOODNESS	quality of wood
WOODNOTE	natural musical note
WOODROOF	plant
WOODSIA	fern
WOODSIER	more connected with woods
WOODSKIN	canoe made of bark
WOODTONE	colour matching that of wood
WOODWALE	green woodpecker
WOODWARD	person in charge of wood
WOODWOSE	hairy wild man of the woods

ANTI- as a prefix gives rise to plenty of high-probability 7s and 8s – the meanings are mainly self-explanatory:

ANTIACNE

ANTIBOSS

ANTICOLD

ANTIDORA (bread used in Russian Orthodox Communion)

ANTIFOG

ANTIGANG

ANTIJAM

ANTIKING (a rival to an established king)

ANTILEAK

ANTIMALE

ANTINUKE

ANTIPOT

ANTIROCK (preventing a vehicle from rocking)

ANTISNOB

ANTITAX

ANTIVAX (opposed to vaccination)

ANTIWEED

Cheating is a very tricky subject to cover. If you're just playing a casual game at home with a like-minded individual, cheating can be fun. However, if there is any degree of competitiveness involved – DON'T CHEAT – it will only end in tears.

The obvious way to cheat is to take a very subtle peep in the bag while (hopefully) your adversary is not looking – you can avoid this by insisting the bag stays above your shoulder when picking tiles. There are all sorts of house rules to combat any shenanigans, but in tournament play there have been several instances of players being banned when caught cheating.

In one event, the deathly hush of the playing area was interrupted by the organiser announcing in front of 200 people that someone had been found out – he was literally frogmarched out of the room by a security guard, never to be seen again...

Obviously, friendly games are a different matter, but if there's any potential of upsetting your opponent rather than humouring them, don't bother.

In any case bad karma will get you in the end.

It can be easy to tell whether your opponent has a good or bad rack by the look on their face once they've picked their tiles, and they can give away where they want to play their next move by staring at a particular part of the board.

This doesn't matter too much in a friendly game but, if you want to win, it will help your cause to watch out for the giveaway signs, and not react to your own letters either facially or verbally.

I think ironically I played a lot better in the 1997 World Championship when I came 5th than when I won in 1993. The biggest mistake I remember making was not missing a good word, but when spotting a difficult winning move VOUGE (not vogue) in a vital game which seemed lost, I got over excited and my body language gave away the fact I thought I could win. My opponent, the legendary American Joe Edley, whose turn it was, later told me that if I had kept a poker face, he would not have caught on to the fact I could win the game – instead he knew I was up to something, spent extra time looking for the move he knew I'd spotted, eventually saw VOUGE, made the necessary block and won the game – very clever.

Try studying these to some degree:

AEROLOGY	study of the atmosphere
AGROLOGY	" " soils
AREOLOGY	Mars
APIOLOGY	bees
BATOLOGY	brambles
CETOLOGY	whales
CHAOLOGY	chaos theory
DEMOLOGY	demography
DOXOLOGY	short hymn
ENOLOGY	study of wine
ETIOLOGY	" " causes of diseases
FETOLOGY	the foetus
MENOLOGY	religious calendar
MISOLOGY	hatred of reasoned argument
MIXOLOGY	the art of mixing cocktails
NOOLOGY	study of intuition
NOMOLOGY	" " law
NOSOLOGY	classification of diseases
OENOLOGY	more wine
OINOLOGY	even more wine
OOLOGY	birds' eggs
OREOLOGY	mountains

PEDOLOGY	children
PELOLOGY	mud therapy
PENOLOGY	punishment
RHEOLOGY	matter in physics
SEXOLOGY	human sexual behaviour
SINOLOGY	Chinese culture
SITOLOGY	food
UFOLOGY	UFOs
VINOLOGY	vines
VIROLOGY	viruses

OLOGY itself is also perfectly acceptable – it has a rather less cerebral anagram.

44 Suffixes

Here are twenty combinations to look out for and
put at the end of your rack since they are very fruitful
suffixes:

-ABLE

-AGE

-ATE

-ED

-ER

-IC

-IEST

-ING

-ISM

-ISE

-ITE

-IVE

-IZE

-LESS

-LY

-MAN

-MEN

-NESS

-OUS

-TION

Apart from the blank, s is the best letter in the Scrabble set, since it starts and ends more words than any other. It should be savoured and ideally kept back to use in a bonus-word – certainly try not to use it unless you can score over 30 points. A good guide is to play it only if the score using it is at least 10 points more than the best score without.

Bear in mind though that multiple Ss on your rack can hold you up. They're not as good together as you may think and if you have two it's normally best to offload one as soon as you can – you should still be able to achieve this with a decent score, but do hold the remaining one back for something special later.

46 Non-words

There's a multitude of surprisingly allowable **non**-words:

NONACTOR	person who is not an actor
NONBANK	business providing similar services to a bank
NONCOLA	soft drink other than cola
NONDRUG	not involving use of drugs
NONELITE	not elite
NONFUEL	not relating to fuel
NONGUILT	innocence
NONHARDY	fragile
NONIMAGE	person who is not a celebrity
NONJURY	trial without a jury
NONLEAFY	not leafy
NONMETRO	not metropolitan
NONNEWS	not concerned with the news
NONOILY	not oily
NONPARTY	not connected with a political party
NONQUOTA	not included in a quota
NONRIGID	not rigid
NONSELF	foreign molecule in the body
NONTIDAL	not having a tide
NONURBAN	rural
NONVITAL	not vital
NONWAGE	not part of wages
NONZERO	not equal to zero
NONWORDS	is in the official Scrabble word list as well.

Play to the Board

A common error among players is to spend all their time looking at their rack rather than the board. It's all very well spotting great words with the tiles in front of you but not much use if there's nowhere to place them. You're far better off spending 90% of your time focusing on the board and its possibilities, trying to keep your letters in your head simultaneously if you can.

Adapting to this '**visual switch**' is very important and can save you a lot of brain energy as well as improve your game. It's not a simple change to achieve, so keep consciously trying to 'catch yourself on' when overfocusing on your rack.

Block when ahead, open when behind. That's the general rule. However, you need to be careful you don't sacrifice too many points just to block, or you may find your lead diminishes sooner than you think. Likewise, you need to open up carefully and too small a score may leave your deficit too great.

Ideally, if you can block and score over 20 points simultaneously when ahead it's worth doing; if you're behind and can open the board for at least 15 points then go for it.

Unlike chess where you have to think about twenty moves ahead, Scrabble is all about maximising your score over your current move as well as the potential score on the next move. This can be achieved with good **rack balancing** to edge you towards that elusive 50-point bonus word, and **set-up** plays.

If you have a high-scoring J, Q, X or Z for example, and nowhere really worthwhile to play it, you may be able to set up a big score next turn by placing one of your vowels next to a premium square. Alternatively, you could set up a hook by holding back a letter that goes on the beginning or end of the word you play.

For example, if you have GHORTUZ, it might be worth playing ROUGH keeping back the T for the front hook next time (it goes on the end as well) – even better if there is a premium square adjacent to the O of ROUGH to set up ZO for an alternative big score next time.

Try not to make the set-up too obvious though and play straight into the hands of your opponent. It's all about giving yourself future opportunities and when they come off it's extremely satisfying.

Knowing your **hooks** can give you a great advantage over your adversary. Here's an A to Z of great front hooks of two-letter words:

A-ZO	containing the divalent group N:N	K-HI	Greek letter
		L-AH	sixth degree of music scale
B-OH	exclamation to startle someone	M-HO	SI unit of conductance
C-HE	pronoun meaning 'I'	N-OX	nitrogen oxide
		O-BE	Laconian village
D-IT	to stop something happening	P-AX	kiss of peace
		Q-IS	energies
		R-EM	dose of radiation
E-ME	uncle	S-HA	be quiet
F-OY	loyalty	T-EF	African grass
G-IF	a file held in GIF format	U-DO	Japanese plant
		V-IN	French wine
H-EH	exclamation of surprise	W-OF	fool
		X-IS	Greek letters
I-TA	type of palm	Y-GO	archaic past participle of 'go'
J-OR	movement in Indian music	Z-EL	Turkish cymbal

There are some surprising hooks you can play on the end of regular two-letter words as well:

GO-A	Tibetan gazelle	WE-M	womb
MI-B	a marble	GO-N	geometrical grade
TO-C	signal for letter T	EX-O	excellent
LO-D	logarithm	HE-P	hip
HI-E	to hurry	LA-R	young man
DO-F	stupid	BY-S	byes
ME-G	megabyte	AT-T	Siamese coin
NO-H	Japanese drama	AM-U	unit of mass
MO-I	me	PA-V	pavlova
HA-J	Muslim pilgrimage	MA-W	to bite
TA-K	take	SO-X	socks
DO-L	unit of pain intensity	HO-Y	to drive animal with cry
		RE-Z	reservation

The only three-letter word ending in Q is SUQ – a Muslim market place – sadly this isn't a hook as SU isn't a word, but it's still extremely useful.

This list of three-vowelled four-letter words will solve
your vowel-heavy rack problems quickly and save you
scoring measly amounts for several turns in a row:

AIGA	family
AINE	male elder
AITU	half-human half-divine being
AJEE	awry
ALAE	wings
AMIA	fish
AUNE	measure of length
AWEE	for a short time
EALE	Roman beast
EAVE	to form eaves
EINA	exclamation of pain
EINE	eyes
EMEU	emu
EOAN	relating to the dawn
ETUI	small ornamented case
EUGE	well done
EVOE	cry of Bacchic frenzy
HUIA	extinct New Zealand bird
IDEE	idea
ILIA	plural of 'ilium'

IURE	by law
KAIE	key
MEOU	to meow
MOAI	Easter Island stone figures
MOOI	pleasing
NAOI	ancient temples
OBIA	a spell
ODEA	buildings for musical performances
OGEE	moulding
OHIA	Hawaiian plant
ONIE	any
OUMA	grandmother
OUPA	grandfather
OWIE	minor injury
PAUA	New Zealand shellfish
QUAI	quay
TOEA	monetary unit of Papua New Guinea
UNAI	two-toed sloth
URAO	mineral
UVAE	grapes
UVEA	part of the eyeball
VIAE	roads
ZOEA	crab larva

SUB- gives rise to some under-ful words:

SUBAREA	area within a larger area
SUBBREED	breed within a larger breed
SUBCOOL	to make colder
SUBDWARF	star smaller than a dwarf star
SUBERECT	not quite erect
SUBFLOOR	rough floor
SUBGOAL	secondary goal
SUBHEAD	heading of a subsection
SUBIDEA	secondary idea
SUBLEVEL	subdivision of a level
SUBMENU	further options within computer menu
SUBNICHE	subdivision of a niche
SUBOCEAN	beneath the ocean
SUBPANEL	panel that is part of a larger panel
SUBRACE	a race considered to be inferior
SUBSONG	subdued birdsong
SUBTUNIC	garment worn under a tunic
SUBUNIT	distinct part of something larger
SUBVICAR	vicar's assistant
SUBWORLD	underworld
SUBZONE	subdivision of a zone

At whatever level you're playing, it's easy to be a good winner but not so a good loser. Don't get too far away from the fact that Scrabble is fun.

There is nothing wrong with being competitive and wanting to win but, unless you really dislike your opponent, in which case you probably shouldn't be playing them in the first place, there's no reason to be a bad loser.

This is often a maturity issue and young players will grow out of it, hopefully sooner rather than later. Sometimes it helps to learn from a particularly painful defeat. When I played in the World Championship Final in 1999, I was beaten by just one point – it hurt badly and I didn't sleep properly for a year afterwards. Whenever I lose these days, I look back and think it can't be as bad as that, and that makes me lose better.

It really isn't worth getting too worked up over – keep things in perspective and enjoy the game whatever the outcome.

Nigel Richards, the world's best player, says he actually doesn't care whether he wins or loses, so long as he enjoys the game – nuff said.

If you think your opponent is capable of some underhand tactics, try some of these to give them a taste of their own medicine:

(a) Make sure they are positioned in front of a mirror so you can see what's on their rack

(b) Party hard the night before and burp alcohol fumes over them

(c) Flick bogeys in the bag to put them off when picking their tiles

(d) Click your knuckles

(e) Cough a lot

(f) Eat lots of garlic

(g) Don't wash for a month before the game

(h) Hum

(i) Grind teeth

(j) Eat baked beans and cauliflower before the game and shoot off some silent-but-violents

I must thank my siblings for these suggestions – I would never have thought of them myself.

It really is surprising how much the official Scrabble word list likes -LIKE as a suffix and it leads to loads of unlikely and useful words, for instance:

AUNTLIKE	MAPLIKE
BAGLIKE	NIBLIKE
CAGELIKE	OWLLIKE
DUNELIKE	PEALIKE
EARLIKE	QUAYLIKE
FATLIKE	RODLIKE
GATELIKE	SAWLIKE
HEADLIKE	TEALIKE
IVYLIKE	URNLIKE
JAWLIKE	VASELIKE
LAVALIKE	WIGLIKE

and I like YLIKE (a Spenserian form of alike) – an anagram of KYLIE who plays apparently – she's also in the dictionary meaning a boomerang. She must be a tough opponent as she'll always come back at you.

Nothing can be more annoying than playing your turn and then spotting a better move that you could have played immediately after when it's too late – but there's a great skill in not compounding the mistake by dwelling on it.

Your mind should be fully focused on your current move and not hampered by wondering what might have been. I remember a Mastermind contestant who was doing brilliantly at the general knowledge round – he whizzed off ten answers in a row, then made one error which threw him completely and he got the next ten wrong.

It's much the same in Scrabble – far better to put mistakes out of your mind and move on.

There are plenty of attributes that go into making a good Scrabble player. Numeracy, literacy, a sound mind, enthusiasm and positivity are just some of them. Experience counts a great deal too: like everything, practice makes perfect and the more you play, the more you'll improve.

A 'killer instinct' is important if you want to take it more seriously – I hope I'm not being too controversial by saying that this tends to be inbred in men more than women, but the reason the stats show that men seem to do better is that they generally have more time on their hands.

Creatives do well at Scrabble – no coincidence that CREATIVES is an anagram of VISCERATE meaning instinctive. Previous World Champions have included a piano teacher, an architect, a top poker player and a TV producer – comedians and musicians are often good players – they attract the same ingredients of brilliant madness.

Here are twenty-six tasty treats using the J:

JA	yes	JEFE	military leader
JO	sweetheart	JEON	Korean pancake
GJU	Shetland violin	JIAO	Chinese currency
TAJ	Muslim cap	JIVY	lively
BAJU	Malay jacket	JOCO	joke
BENJ	Indian hemp	JOTA	Spanish dance
DOJO	judo hall	JUBE	church gallery
GAJO	non-gypsy	JYNX	woodpecker
JAAP	simpleton (*South*	FALAJ	water channel
	African offensive)	KANJI	Japanese writing
JAGA	to guard		system
JAKE	all right	LAPJE	rag
JAXY	buttocks	NDUJA	spicy pork paste
JEAT	jet	PUNJI	bamboo stick

Ideally you'll be looking to use the J in conjunction with one of the premium squares, and scoring around thirty points in the process if the board is relatively open.

JINN is a spirit (not the drink) in Muslim mythology, but it can be spelt in several different ways:

DJIN

DJINN

DJINNI

DJINNY

GINN

JINNEE

JINNI

Of these, only DJIN, DJINN, JINN and JINNI take an S for some reason.

To confuse you further, also allowable are JIN – a Chinese unit of weight – and JINNE, which is a South African exclamation of surprise.

The Q can really cramp your style during the game and it's really not worth holding on to in the hope that you pick up a U further down the line. However, as well as the invaluable QI, there are some more wonderful U-less Q words. These are the most useful ones:

QAT	African shrub
QIN	Chinese musical instrument
CINQ	number five
FIQH	Islamic jurisprudence
QADI	Muslim judge
QAID	chief
QOPH	Hebrew letter
WAQF	Muslim endowment
FAQIR	Muslim who spurns worldly possessions
NIQAB	Muslim veil
QANAT	underground channel
QAPIK	Azerbaijani monetary unit
QIBLA	direction of Mecca
QORMA	mild Indian dish
TALAQ	Muslim divorce
TRANQ	tranquilizer

NIQAAB	Muslim veil
QABALA	Jewish mystical tradition
QASIDA	Arabic verse form
QIGONG	system of breathing and exercise
QINDAR	Albanian monetary unit
QINTAR	Albanian monetary unit
QWERTY	keyboard
SHEQEL	Israeli monetary unit
YAQONA	Polynesian shrub
INQILAB	revolution

The X is the best of the high-scorers, largely because it goes with all the vowels to make two-letter words:

AX   axe
EX   to delete
XI   Greek letter
OX
XU   Vietnamese currency

Always look to play it on the doubles and triples – doubling up both ways can bring you an easy thirty-two or tripling gets you 48 points just for the X alone.

Here are some three-letter X-amples to help you X-cel:

DEX   dextroamphetamine
DOX   to publish someone's personal information on the internet
DUX   top school pupil
GOX   gaseous oxygen
HOX   hamstring
KEX   plant
LEX   system of laws
LOX   to load with liquid oxygen
MUX   to spoil
OXY   ox

PIX   receptacle
PYX   receptacle
REX   king
TEX   weight unit measuring yarn density
TIX   tickets
TUX   tuxedo
VAX   vaccination
VOX   voice
WEX   to wax
WOX   wax
YEX   to hiccup

The infamous **ZO** – officially a Tibetan breed of cattle formed by crossing a yak with a cow – has ten other members of its herd:

DSO

DSOBO

DSOMO

DZO

DZHO

JOMO

ZHO

ZHOMO

ZOBO

ZOBU

Note well that the **DSOMO** and **ZHOMO** are female, while the **ZEBU** – an Asian ox with a humped back – can be seen grazing in the next field.

When you happen to spot a fantastic word or a game-winning move, just take a minute or so to savour the satisfaction, rather than play it immediately.

The uplifting feeling will seep through you – you don't have to jump in the air or do handstands – just sit back and relax in your good vibe, whilst your opponent has absolutely no idea what's coming.

Lots of South African entries have reached the official Scrabble word list in the last few years, for example:

BRU	a friend
JOL	to have a good time
SIF	nasty
BOEP	protruding belly
BOET	brother
BRAK	crossbred dog
EISH	expressing dismay
ISIT	seeking confirmation
KAAL	naked
KIFF	excellent
MOER	to attack someone
WENA	you
YEBO	yes
BRAAI	to grill over open coals
NOOIT	expressing surprise
SPAZA	township shop (*slang*)
VOEMA	vigour

There are loads of handy front hooks of three-letter words to make some really weird four-letter words – here's just a sample:

S-AXE	greyish-blue colour	G-LEG	quick
K-BAR	kilobar	S-MEW	a duck
E-COD	expression of surprise	E-NOW	enough
		Y-OWE	ewe
U-DON	Japanese noodles	A-POD	animal without feet
T-EGG	two-year-old sheep	E-REV	day before
		V-ROT	rotten
V-EGO	vegetarian	V-ROW	woman
M-EVE	to move	E-SKY	food and drink container
A-GIN	against		
P-HAT	terrific	E-THE	easy
Z-ILL	finger cymbal	O-URN	our
J-IMP	handsome	E-VET	newt
T-IVY	at full speed	H-WAN	won
S-JOE	exclamation of surprise	H-YEN	hyena
		P-YET	magpie
K-LAP	to slap	M-ZEE	old person

A Young Man's Game?

Fourteen of the fifteen World Champions have been single men under forty years old. Joel Wapnick from Canada gives hope to us all – he won the title at the age of fifty-three – but there's no denying agile young minds have an advantage. The best young players are from Pakistan and Thailand as Scrabble is included in their school curriculum, as it is in Nigeria, as a way of teaching English. It would be lovely to see a greater Scrabble presence in UK schools as it's such a fun way to improve children's literacy and numeracy.

There are a few youth workshops and competitions over here. Having personally taught in several lunchtime and after-school clubs, I can say that the enthusiasm is tremendous. A word of advice, however, to the youngsters from a wise old man: 'don't be too cocky and slow down a bit'.

Another alphabet of absolute beauties:

ADZUKI	leguminous plant
BLIPVERT	very short television advertisement
CHILIDOG	hot dog with chilli sauce
DRONKLAP	drunkard
EXEQUY	funeral rite
FJELD	high rocky Scandinavian plateau
GILLYVOR	carnation
HRYVNIA	money unit of Ukraine
IZVESTIA	news
JEDI	person claiming to live according to Star Wars Jedi philosophy
KUVASZ	Hungarian dog
LOGJUICE	poor quality port
MPRET	former Albanian ruler
NONG	stupid person (*Australian slang*)
OULAKAN	fish
PYENGADU	leguminous tree
QUANDONG	small Australian tree
RUBABOO	soup
STINKPOT	person that stinks

TAKIN	massive South Asian mammal with shaggy coat and backwards and upwards horns
UINTAITE	asphalt
VOZHD	Russian leader
WAYLEGGO	'away here! let go!'
XENOPUS	African frog
YUTZ	fool
ZELATRIX	nun monitoring younger nuns' behaviour

-FISH is another swimmingly seaworthy suffix when you trawl through the official Scrabble word list:

BATFISH	MILKFISH
CAVEFISH	NUMBFISH
DEALFISH	OARFISH
FOOLFISH	PANFISH
GOATFISH	ROSEFISH
HEADFISH	STUDFISH
JEWFISH	TUBFISH
LADYFISH	WEAKFISH

The de-fin-itions are not in plaice: they're all types of fish.

Tracking tiles is allowable and really important if you want to get more serious. It helps to give you a rough idea of consonant to vowel ratio as the game goes on. If you find more consonants than normal have already been played for example, you may want to play less on your turn as there are comparatively less left in the bag to pick – this is really useful when it comes to balancing your rack.

However, the main point of tracking is in the endgame, especially if the scores are close. If you track correctly – which is surprisingly simple with a bit of practice – you will know what's on your opponent's rack once the bag is emptied. This allows you to spot what you think is their best move and stop them in their tracks by blocking appropriately, which could make all the difference between winning and losing.

All you need to do to tile track is write out the alphabet at the start of the game and cross off the letters as they are played. For example, if MARK is played on the first move, write down 8 next to your A as there will be eight A's left unplayed. Similarly 1 next to the M, 5 next to the R and delete the K completely.

If you keep going, and cross out your own rack once the bag is empty, you should be left with exactly what's on your opponent's rack.

71 | Check Your Averages

You can get a good idea as to how fast your game is improving by working out your average score per (two-player) game – even more useful is finding your average move score.

As a rough guide, you're doing well if you score 300, while 300–350 will see you hold your own at a club, and 350–400 will stand you in good stead at an event. The top players average 400–450.

Scores can vary dramatically depending on the state of the board (open or blocked) and the quality of opponent, which is why average move score is a better indicator. Aim for over 20 points per move – 25 is really good and 30 is excellent.

Doing this can give you a good feel for what to look for from each turn. For instance, if you can only find a score less than 20 points, it might be worth considering changing your letters unless the ones you hold back are so good that you're likely to make up for it with a score of 30–40 on the next turn.

The odd one out of ENGLAND, IRELAND, SCOTLAND and WALES is IRELAND, as it's the only one not to have an anagram – surprising with such common letters.

ENGLAND	ENDLANG	lengthways
SCOTLAND	COTLANDS	cotter's grounds
WALES	ALEWS	hunting cries
	SWALE	to sway
	SWEAL	to scorch
	WEALS	raised skin marks

However, IRELAND does go with the following letters to make an eight-letter word:

+B	BILANDER	small cargo ship
+E	RENAILED	
+F	FILANDER	kangaroo
+G	DANGLIER	
+G	DEARLING	
+G	DRAGLINE	
+H	HARDLINE	
+N	INLANDER	
+S	ISLANDER	

There's a plethora of Māori words in the official Scrabble word list – here are some really useful 4s:

HAKU	the kingfish
HAPU	a subtribe
HIOI	plant of the mint family
HOKA	red cod
KARO	small shrub
KAWA	protocol
KETE	basket
KOHA	gift
KORU	carving pattern
KUIA	elderly woman
KUTU	body louse
MIHA	young fern
MIHI	to greet ceremonially
MIRO	coniferous tree
NAMU	black sandfly
PATU	short club
PUHA	sow thistle
PUKA	tobacco plant
ROHE	tribal territory
WERO	challenge
WHIO	blue duck

Here's a top twenty of Māori 5s – they can often get you out of vowel trouble:

AINGA	village
ARIKI	first-born child
AROHA	love
HIKOI	to protest
HINAU	tree
KANAE	grey mullet
KAURU	edible cabbage stem
KAWAU	black shag
KEHUA	ghost
KIORE	rat
KOURA	crayfish
MAPAU	small tree
MATAI	evergreen tree
MAURI	the soul
MOHUA	small bird
PIKAU	rucksack
POTAE	hat
RAHUI	prohibition
RAUPO	bulrush
TAWAI	beech

75 | Type-cast

There are several kinds of words with the -TYPE suffix:

AUTOTYPE	photographic process
BIOTYPE	genetically identical plant group
CEROTYPE	printing plate process
ECOTYPE	group of organisms
GENOTYPE	genetic constitution of organism
HOLOTYPE	original specimen
IDIOTYPE	unique part of antibody
KALOTYPE	early photographic process
LINOTYPE	line of metal type
MONOTYPE	single print
NEOTYPE	replacement specimen
OVERTYPE	to type over existing text
PRETYPE	to type in advance
SEROTYPE	category into which bacterium is placed
TINTYPE	photographic print
VARITYPE	to produce copy
ZOOTYPE	animal figure used as a symbol

Don't give up if you find yourself a long way behind; part of the beauty of Scrabble is there's nearly always the opportunity to turn it around.

When I was playing in the World Championship Final, I was 177 down and came back to win by 7 points to make the match score 2–2. My opponent was so downhearted that the deciding game was a breeze. Keep positive and believe the 'tile gods' will ultimately favour you – you'll be surprised how often they do.

If you are really keen, you could record all sorts of word lists and play them back to yourself with some uplifting background music. You'll be surprised how many will subconsciously stick.

But beware: this form of practice can be highly dangerous. You would think that long car journeys would be an ideal opportunity to make use of this method, but in my experience you have a high chance of falling asleep at the wheel. Therefore, playback time might be best left for going to bed; it's a great cure for insomnia if nothing else.

If you're ahead in the game, there are some great six-letter words that are especially useful in acting as blockers as they don't take any hooks at either end. Also, the more letters you play when in front, the sooner you get to the finishing line. Here's an alphabet of examples:

ARGULI	parasites on fish	MARAKA	Bosnia-Herzegovina unit of currency
BONZER	excellent		
CHANGA	expression of approval	NOGAKU	Japanese drama
DADGUM	damned	OCHONE	expression of regret
EQUALI	pieces for instruments	PLONGD	plunged
FOOBAR	irreparably damaged	QUOOKE	quaked
		ROTOLI	Italian roll
GATVOL	fed up	SHAZAM	magic slogan
HEARIE	hairy	TIGLIC	syrupy liquid
IBIDEM	in the same place	UBIQUE	everywhere
		VERLIG	enlightened
JANTEE	sprightly	WABBIT	weary
KEIGHT	two-masted sailing vessel	XOANON	carved image of a god
LIKUTA	coin in the former Zaïre	YITTEN	frightened
		ZAFTIG	curvaceous

They have the added advantage of potentially lulling your opponent into a mistake by putting an S on the end and thereby losing a turn.

ETAERIO – a kind of fruit – is the most likely seven-letter bonus word to appear on your rack. Here's a taster of some more fruitful seven-letter words made up of the letters you are most likely to draw: ADEILNORST. They are especially useful when they have no anagram and are listed here in order of probability of being drawn:

ERASION	act of erasing	ALIENER	one who transfers
ATONIES	lack of muscle tone	EATERIE	restaurant
EROTISE	to make erotic	ARENOSE	sandy
AIERIES	eagles' nests	OLEATES	salts of oleic acid
TAENIAE	ancient Greek headbands	TORNADE	tornado
INOSITE	alcohol	AEOLIAN	relating to the wind
ROSEATE	rose-coloured		
SEALINE	sailing company	OREADES	mountain nymphs
SENARII	poems	SIENITE	igneous rock
ANISOLE	colourless liquid	INEDITA	unpublished writings
ESTRONE	hormone	AEROSAT	communications satellite
OLEARIA	daisy bush		
RIOTISE	riotous behaviour	TENENDA	parts of terms of tenure

AERATION – putting gas into a liquid – is the most commonly played eight-letter word in Scrabble. You'll be surprised how often the following words appear if you hold the right bonus-conducive letters back:

INERTIAE	a plural of 'inertia'	ORIENTED	orientated
ERIONITE	glassy mineral	AURELIAN	person who studies butterflies
AEROLITE	meteorite	DELATION	bringing a charge against
AEROTONE	bath with air jets		
ERADIATE	radiate	INAURATE	gilded
DENTARIA	botanical term	NOTITIAE	ecclesiastical registers
DOUANIER	customs officer	ETOURDIE	foolish
TENORITE	black mineral	RITORNEL	orchestral passage
TAENIATE	ribbon-like	RETINOID	vitamin A derivative
ETIOLATE	to become weak		
LITERATO	literary person	TERATOID	like a monster
TENTORIA	membranes	INTORTED	twisted inward
RETAILOR	to tailor afresh	TRIENNIA	periods of three years

Here are thirty bizarre end hooks to normal three-letter words that make perfectly valid 4s:

BAG-H	garden	NAB-K	edible berry
BED-U	relating to bedouins	PAW-A	peacock
		PUT-Z	to waste time
COX-A	hipbone	ROT-L	unit of weight
DID-O	antic	SEX-T	noon
FEE-B	contemptible person	SIT-Z	bath
		TOY-O	Japanese material for making hats
FIX-T	fixed		
GEE-Z	expression of surprise		
		TRY-E	very good
GET-A	Japanese sandal	UPS-Y	drunken merry-making
HER-Y	to praise		
IMP-I	group of Zulu warriors	VAN-G	rope on ship
		VAT-U	monetary unit of Vanuatu
JAM-B	to climb a crack in a rock		
		WAD-T	wad
KIP-E	basket for catching fish	WET-A	wingless insect
		YES-K	to hiccup
LIP-O	liposuction	YOU-K	to itch
MAR-Y	marijuana	ZIT-I	pasta

These four-vowelled five-letter words are rare in normal English but extremely useful in Scrabble:

AECIA	structures in fungi
AERIE	eagle's nest
AQUAE	waters
AULOI	ancient Greek pipes
AURAE	a plural of 'aura'
AUREI	Roman coins
LOOIE	lieutenant
LOUIE	"
MIAOU	to meow
OORIE	shabby
OUIJA	spirit board
OURIE	shabby
URAEI	sacred Egyptian serpents
ZOAEA	crab larva
ZOOEA	" "

The triple-word squares – TWS – are the most bountiful on the board when it comes to points potential. When one becomes available it's often the place to play, but don't get too transfixed by a triple. Some opportunities are better than others depending on your letters. So think very carefully before playing a vowel immediately adjacent to a TWS, but placing a low scoring consonant on the triple line isn't as dangerous as you might think.

Your opponent might score thirty or so points off it, but that's worth the risk if your triple opening move scores far better than any other on the board. You might get unlucky and let them in for a big fifty-plus score, or in the worst-case scenario a **triple-triple** or '**9-timer**', where they place their seven letters around the one you've put on the triple line to take in two TWS's for a mammoth move – I once scored 311 with CONQUEST. This, however, occurs very rarely and the trick is not to be too paranoid.

So weigh up the odds when opening a TWS – it's worth doing if your score outweighs the give away potential.

If it's your move and a TWS is available, it's the first place you look for, but if you can't make the most of it, don't be afraid to look elsewhere – your opponent may not be able to use it effectively either. An interesting tactic in this instance is to open up a second TWS so you get a share of the spoils on your next turn – risky but fun.

There are plenty of Delhi-cious short words originating from India:

DAK	mail	GORI	white female (*Hinglish Informal*)
GHI	ghee	GYAN	knowledge
JAI	victory	KHUD	ravine
REH	salty crust on soil	KUTA	male dog
SER	unit of weight	KUTI	female dog
URD	bean	LAKH	100,000
ANNA	coin	LEEP	to plaster with cow-dung
ARNA	water buffalo	MALA	string of beads used in prayer
ARTI	religious ritual		
BABU	Mister	MOTI	fat woman
BAEL	spiny tree	MOWA	tree
BAPU	spiritual father	NACH	dance
BHUT	ghost	NALA	ravine
BUDA	old man	PICE	coin
BUDI	old woman	RYOT	peasant
CHIK	a blind	SANT	devout person
DESI	authentic	TEEK	well
DHOL	drum	YAAR	friend
GORA	white male (*Hinglish Informal*)	ZILA	administrative district

Have a Goa at these Indian 5s:

AARTI	ceremony with lighted candles
BAJRA	cereal grass
BUNDH	strike
BEEDI	hand-rolled cigarette
BIGHA	land measure
CHOLI	blouse
DHABA	roadside cafe
DHUTI	loincloth
DURZI	tailor
GOSHT	meat dish
JAGRA	festival
JOWAR	grass
KHADI	cotton cloth
LUNGI	long cloth
MANDI	big market
PIPUL	fig tree
RATHA	carriage
SWAMI	mystic
TAVAH	frying pan
THAGI	thuggery
TONGA	two-wheeled vehicle
YOJAN	unit of distance

Apart from some of the major events where there's a 5-point penalty, you've got nothing to lose in UK Scrabble by challenging a word you don't know, whereas in the US you lose your next turn if the word turns out to be OK. There's something aesthetically unpleasing about nonwords staying on the board, but it's surprising how often it happens.

Don't be afraid to challenge: if you have a scintilla of doubt, look it up. There's nothing more frustrating than letting a word go and finding it's not in the dictionary when it's too late. It might seem obvious when the challenges are 'free', but it's surprising how often players feel too embarrassed or intimidated to check.

As a general rule, challenge anything you wouldn't be sure of playing yourself.

Vs are horrible and should be discarded at the earliest opportunity. Here are forty voluptuous three- and four-letter V-words to assist you:

DEV	divine being
EVO	evening
LUV	love
SAV	saveloy
UVA	grape
VAC	to vacuum
VAV	Hebrew letter
VAW	Hebrew letter
VIG	interest on loan
VOE	small bay
VOL	heraldic wings
VOR	to warn
VUG	small rock cavity
VUM	to swear
GYVE	to shackle
KAVA	Polynesian shrub
OMOV	'one member, one vote'
RIVO	informal toast
TAVA	Indian frying pan
ULVA	seaweed
VAGI	cranial nerves
VANG	rope on ship

VAUT	vault
VEEP	vice president
VEHM	medieval German court
VERD	marble
VEXT	vexed
VIBS	climbing shoes
VILD	vile
VITE	musical direction
VIVA	to examine in a spoken interview
VIVE	long live
VIVO	with vigour
VIZY	to look
VLEI	low marshy ground
VOLK	nation
VRIL	life force
VROU	woman
VUGH	small rock cavity
VULN	to wound

Two letters that are awful together are the U and W – there are a few words to help get rid of them both in one turn:

WUD	wood
WUS	term of address
WAUK	full cloth
WAUL	to cry like a cat
WAUR	war
WHUP	to defeat totally
WUDU	ritual washing
WULL	will
DWAUM	to faint
SWOUN	swoon
UNWED	not wed
UNWET	not wet
UNWIT	to divest of wit
UNWON	not won
VROUW	woman
WAUFF	to flutter
WAUGH	to bark
WAULK	full cloth
WHUMP	to make a dull thud
WOFUL	woeful
WUDDY	loop at end of rope
WURST	large sausage
WUSHU	Chinese martial arts
WUSSY	feeble
WUXIA	Chinese film

There are also some wonderful words using the prefix SUPER-. Here are a few examples of eight-letter words that may help get you that elusive 50-point bonus (you can guess the definitions!):

SUPERBAD

SUPERCAR

SUPERCOW

SUPERFAN

SUPERGUN

SUPERHOT

SUPERJET

SUPERLOO

SUPERMOM

SUPERSET

SUPERSPY

ANGRIEST is the most productive eight-letter anagram combination:

ANGSTIER   more anxious
ASTRINGE   to cause contraction
GANISTER   sedimentary rock
GANTRIES
GRANITES
INGRATES   ungrateful people
RANGIEST
REASTING   being noisily uncooperative
STEARING   steering
TASERING   using a Taser gun

It's not that important to know all the anagrams – the more the better – but if you know two or three, you're more than likely to be able to fit one of them on the board.

A few -WISE words to end our suffix sojourn:

ARCHWISE	like an arch
BENDWISE	diagonally
CRABWISE	sideways
DROPWISE	in form of a drop
EDGEWISE	edgeways
FANWISE	like a fan
LONGWISE	lengthways
MANWISE	in a human way
OVERWISE	too wise
PALEWISE	by perpendicular lines
RINGWISE	experienced in the ring
SOMEWISE	to some degree
TENTWISE	in the manner of a tent
WARPWISE	in the direction of the warp

Interestingly, WISEMAN is not allowed but WISEWOMAN is – it means a witch.

PATERNAL has two appropriate anagrams –
PARENTAL and PRENATAL – speaking of which
there's also PARLANTE.

Is this coincidence or is there more to it? When you
consider that the following are also anagrams of one
another –

'ELEVEN PLUS TWO' and 'TWELVE PLUS ONE'

'APPLE MACINTOSH' and 'LAPTOP MACHINES'

'THE HOUSES OF PARLIAMENT' and 'LOONIES FAR
UP THE THAMES'

– and the fact that the only time I've ever, in tens of
thousands of games, played NY and MAN in the same
move, was in the World Championship Final – in New
York… you start to wonder – well I certainly do.

Respect your opponent by not playing too slowly. A good average time to play each move is about two minutes. In tournament play, special timers are used and you're allowed twenty-five minutes to play all your moves – since each game lasts an average of about thirteen moves each, you're looking at just under two minutes for each turn.

Some moves are more difficult than others, so it's fair enough to take longer sometimes, but anything in excess of five minutes and you're likely to send your opponent to sleep.

If you use a timer, the rule is that you lose 10 points for every minute (or part thereof) that you go over the twenty-five minute deadline. There was a rather elderly chap in the States who was 250 points ahead in his game, when he started snoring – his devious opponent realised his only chance of winning was to let him stay asleep and the poor man apparently went over on his timer by twenty-five minutes. He woke up to find that his 250 point lead had been cancelled out, but just in time to play the winning move: justice done.

By the way ZZZS is actually a valid word – the last in the official Scrabble word list – though you'd have to use both blanks to play it as there's only one Z in the set.

The final word on the hooks is left to these fabulous front hooks of seven-letter words to make fantastic 8s:

A-DUSTING	drying up by heat
B-ARTISAN	small turret
C-UNIFORM	ancient writing system
D-HURRIES	Indian cotton carpets
E-RODENTS	things that wear away
F-UGLIEST	extremely ugly
G-ELASTIC	relating to laughter
H-EXAMINE	type of fuel
I-CONICAL	relating to an icon
J-AUNTIES	naval masters-at-arms
K-VETCHES	grumbles
L-IGNEOUS	like wood
M-UNITING	strengthening
N-OVATION	substitution of a new obligation
O-DONATES	dragonflies
P-LUMBAGO	plant
R-ENFORCE	reinforce
S-CHILLER	unusual mineral lustre
T-HERMITS	processes for reducing metallic oxides
U-PLAYING	stashing
V-ROOMING	moving noisily at high speed
W-INDIGOS	cannibals
Y-EARLIES	once a year events
Z-INKIEST	most like zinc

You don't need to wear 666 across your forehead or bring in a black cat, but if you think a certain superstition brings you luck, use it – for the power of positive thinking if nothing else.

When I won the World Championship, I found I was on a winning run after using the same toilet cubicle in between games – I would go through the same routine every time, but it became rather embarrassing when someone was already in there and I hung around the bathroom waiting for them to finish – I remember getting several strange looks from other users of the facilities.

Part of the beauty of Scrabble is that, with some good fortune, nearly anyone can beat anyone. However, luck does not play as big a part in the game as you might think. It is no coincidence that the weakest players are the ones who tend to blame their luck the most.

Nigel Richards, multiple World Champion and regarded by many as the best player in the world, never curses his luck. He has won countless tournaments and almost invariably features in the top five of any event. Skill in Scrabble far outweighs fortune. The more you moan about your letters, the worse they are likely to get – negativity breeds negativity so avoid it at all costs.

You can certainly **make your own luck** in the game by giving yourself opportunities that others might not spot – it doesn't pay off all the time, but it will count in the long run.

The biggest luck element comes in picking up most of the blanks and Ss – the best tiles in the set. Even then, you can increase your chances of getting these by simply playing more letters than your opponent, which is a skill in itself.

Over a lot of games, the better players always rise to the top, but if you're evenly matched, a little bit of luck can make all the difference.

Every five years or so, the official Scrabble word list is updated. The latest edition contains over 3000 new words up to nine letters in length which are recognised in official tournament play.

Forty fabulous new favourites follow:

AMAKHOSI	Zulu clan chiefs
ARANCINI	fried rice balls
BIZJET	small plane used by businesspeople
BLUD	friend (slang)
CATAGEN	phase of hair growth
COTIJA	salty Mexican cheese
DADBOD	untoned male physique
EMBIGGEN	to make bigger
ENCOLPIA	religious symbols worn on breast
FARANG	Thai for a foreigner
FLEEK	as in *on fleek* stylish
GRAWLIX	sequence of symbols in text to replace profanity
GREEBOS	dirty-looking rock music fans
HEIDUC	Hungarian guerilla warrior
HYGGE	Danish practice promoting wellbeing
ILIACI	muscles near the ilium
INDYREF	independence referendum
JOLLOF	West African rice dish

JUGAAD	problem-solving
LABNEH	Mediterranean soft cheese
LISTICLE	article consisting of a list
LOOGIE	lump of spit and phlegm
MALTIPOO	cross between Maltese and poodle
MUZAKIER	having a blander sound
NYAOPE	narcotic substance
OMNIANAS	miscellaneous collections
PECTINEI	thigh muscles
PLOGGING	picking up litter while jogging
PREGGO	pregnant *(slang)*
RENDANG	spicy Indonesian meat dish
SANTOKU	Japanese knife
SKODY	unkempt
TIFO	organised fan display during football match
TITUPIER	livelier
TURNT	intoxicated
UMEBOSHI	dried and pickled Japanese fruit
VEDUTAS	paintings of a town or city
WORDIE	person who loves words
YOWZA	exclamation of enthusiasm
ZOMBOID	like a zombie

...and now it's ok to be OK.

If you are enthusiastic enough to look at some word lists, a good way to study is to remove the words you are sure you have mastered by deleting them with a black marker pen.

Each time you go back to the relevant page, you'll be able to remove more by recognition, so it will continually seem less daunting to study until you ultimately eliminate the whole page – this is a very satisfying and positive way to learn and move on.

If you hold six or seven consonants on your rack, you'll be looking to restore the balance.

These two- and three-letter consonant-only words will help:

CH	eke
FY	fie
KY	cows
NY	nigh
HM	hesitation
MM	enjoyment
BRR	shivering
CLY	to steal
CWM	steep-sided hollow
GYP	to cheat
HMM	more hesitation
HYP	hypotenuse
LYM	leash
MYC	gene causing tumours
PHT	irritation
RHY	rye
SWY	Australian gambling game
SYN	since
TWP	stupid
TYG	mug with two handles
VLY	low marshy ground
WYN	rune equivalent to English *w*

Four- and five-letter words to alleviate a consonant crisis:

BRRR	more shivering	SKYF	to smoke a cigarette
BYRL	to remove lumps in cloth	SKYR	Scandinavian cheese
FYRD	Anglo-Saxon militia	SYPH	syphilis
GYMP	to limp	TRYP	parasite
GYNY	gynaecology	TYMP	blast furnace outlet
HWYL	emotional fervour	TYPP	unit of thickness of yarn
KYND	kind	TYPY	typifying breed of animal
LYCH	dead body		
PFFT	sudden disappearance	WYCH	tree
RYND	crossbar part of millstone	WYND	narrow lane
		WYNN	rune equivalent to English *w*
SCRY	to divine by crystal gazing	XYST	long portico
SKRY	to try to tell future	YMPT	repaired birds' wings

Watch out for CRWTH, an ancient stringed Celtic instrument, and CWTCH – to be snuggled up. There's also the unlikely PHPHT, which expresses irritation.

Anything that gives you a good vibe is worth pursuing. It could be as simple as deciding that AMIGO is a better opening move than its anagram IMAGO, just because it's more user friendly. So be mindful to play positive words, especially ones you'd be happy to describe yourself, or it could come back to haunt you. The superficial papers picked up on the fact that my final move when winning the World Championship was 'WET' – the rather unimaginative headlines went along the lines of 'WET wins World Scrabble Final' – never mind MUTAGENIC etc. In hindsight I wish I had played the harmless alternatives TEW or EWT. If lucky enough to face the same situation again, I definitely wouldn't settle for DUST and would be delighted to play the alternative.

If you're getting eager and fancy trying out an international (English-speaking) Scrabble tournament, I would highly recommend the 'King's Cup' in Bangkok – effectively Thailand's national championship. Held every July, this is an incredible event, open to everyone. It takes place in Bangkok's biggest shopping complex, which is the only place big enough to accommodate the ever-increasing number of participants (it's getting close to 10,000).

There is an opening ceremony which features dancing girls and players welcomed on stage with their national flags. Then there's some pretty intense Scrabble for four days while the atmosphere positively buzzes, culminating in the finalists being serenaded to the sound of Queen's 'We Are the Champions'.

The winner gets a cheque for $10,000 from a member of Thailand's royal family and, if they are sensible, goes for a well-earned rest on one of Thailand's fantastic islands for a couple of weeks.

There's a host of other events on the international calendar – to find out more, take a look at the World English-language Scrabble Players Association (WESPA) website – **www.wespa.org**

103 Over.....

You can get too much of a good thing with some of these:

OVERABLE

OVERBIG

OVERCOY

OVERDUST

OVEREGG

OVERFISH

OVERGILD

OVERHOLY

OVERIDLE

OVERJUST

OVERKNEE

OVERLEWD

OVERMILK

OVERNET

OVERPLUS

OVERRUDE

OVERSUDS

OVERTART

OVERURGE

OVERVEIL

OVERWILY

OVERYEAR

OVERZEAL

Here are some more out-standing words:

OUTADDS

OUTBITCH

OUTCHEAT

OUTDREAM

OUTECHO

OUTFLASH

OUTGNAW

OUTHOWL

OUTJINX

OUTKISS

OUTLOVE

OUTMARCH

OUTNAME

OUTPITY

OUTQUOTE

OUTRING

OUTSIZE

OUTTHROB

OUTVENOM

OUTWHIRL

OUTYELL

You could say they're all OUTASITE.

There are some lovely three-letter words involving the z:

ADZ	adze	WIZ	wizard
BEZ	part of deer's horn	ZAG	to change direction sharply
BIZ	business	ZAX	saxophone
CAZ	casual	ZEA	corn silk
COZ	cousin	ZEE	the letter Z
CUZ	cousin	ZEK	Soviet prisoner
FIZ	fizz	ZEN	calm meditative state
JIZ	wig	ZEP	long sandwich
LUZ	indestructible human bone	ZEX	cutting tool
MIZ	misery	ZIG	to change direction sharply
MOZ	jinx	ZIN	zinfandel
POZ	positive	ZIT	pimple
RIZ	past form of rise	ZOA	independent animal bodies
SAZ	Middle Eastern instrument	ZOL	cannabis cigarette
SEZ	says		
TIZ	state of confusion		

Keep looking to play the z across and down simultaneously on the premium squares – double gets you forty points, triple scores a hefty sixty.

The older I get, the more I believe in Karma. I started thinking things were 'meant to be' after the ludicrous luck I had in winning the World Championship against Joel Wapnick. Six years on it partially evened itself out when I think it's fair to say I was very unlucky in losing to Joel by 1 point in the 1999 Final. It more than evened itself out in the 2016 Final when Brett Smitheram, with a combination of great skill and greater luck, thrashed me – what goes around comes around. So now I think never mind if I have a bad tournament, the next one will be good.

This can even extend to the choices of moves I make – for example if my opponent's first move is BEGONIA and I have HIPORSS, I would prefer ROSEHIPS through the E over the equally nice POSERISH and SPOSHIER just to keep the plant theme going. Even if it scores a few less points than the other two, it's made up for by the satisfaction of going with the flow(er). This may sound mad but I like it – make coincidences happen – SCRABBLE SERENDIPITY.

I used to think that you should stick to your own game regardless of your opponent – I no longer think that's totally true. Some players, notably many of the top Africans, like a very closed game, so I will specially look to play open against them. Nigel Richards, on the other hand, knows pretty much everything, so it's a good tactic to play tight against him to restrict his inevitably better vocabulary. A lot of players lose to Nigel before the game has even started as they're intimidated – not by Nigel who is a nice guy but by his stature as the best player in the history of Scrabble – so they tend to play worse than usual and make mistakes they wouldn't normally make. It's really important to focus on your own game when you're playing a better player. If there's a bit of history between you and your opponent, memories of previous games between you can help – for example if I was to play Brett Smitheram again and I had AIMNOR? and a choice of lots of bonus words, I would definitely go for AMORINI as he missed it against me on the last turn to lose a crucial game a few years back – similarly I'm sure he wouldn't hesitate if he could play BRACONID* over anything else with a similar rack of ACINOR?, as he scored 176 points for it against me in the 2016 World Final.

* a parasitic wasp

It's quite interesting that nearly half the former World Scrabble Champions are no longer active tournament players. I think this has a lot to do with the fact that, once you hit the top, there's nowhere else to go but down. That's why it's good to pick a better player than you to aspire to – it keeps you motivated. My nemesis is Nigel Richards – I may never overcome him but my Scrabble ambition these days is to catch him. As I write he's 28–16 up on me so there's a lot of work to do, but it's gratifying to know that, in my view the greatest sportsman of all time – Roger Federer – is 24–16 down on Rafa Nadal. Maybe wanting to reel in Rafa is a reason Roger keeps going, as well as his genius and genuine love of the game.

Often the most difficult moves to make are those where you are unable to decide between two equally good choices. You can waste lots of time wondering which one to go for so it's good to have a plan in this situation. Personally I would go on gut feeling or if I'm still struggling I'll decide to play the word closer to the end of the dictionary. I prefer Tails to Heads so for example I'll go for FLEEING over FEELING. I used to agonise over whether to keep back an R or T as they seem equally good, so now to save time I'll stick with the R solely because I support QPR (nickname the Rs). I am well into 'out of the box' – some might say 'off your box' – thinking. In my view, the more you think 'out of the box' the more success you'll have in the box.

When I co-produced Channel 4's *Countdown* in the 1990s, all 5 shows were top 5 in the channel's ratings week in week out and regularly attracted 4/5 million viewers. In hindsight this was mainly down to the genius of the presenter Richard Whiteley (RIP), but we also gelled as a team. We could laugh at each other as well as ourselves and I think that was the secret of the show's success. It didn't seem like a job – it was fun so don't forget that Scrabble is just a silly game and meant to be fun. If you take it too seriously, you'll stop enjoying it – what's the point of that?

Making the most of the endgame is worthy of a book in itself. A few principles to follow once the bag is empty are:

(a) Assuming you can't use all your letters in one go, try to find a way of playing out in two turns, to give yourself the best chance of playing the last move of the game.

(b) Score as many points as possible over the two turns, ideally at the same time, stopping your opponent from getting their best score or from playing out (you'll know their letters and what they can potentially play if you've tile tracked correctly).

(c) Think hard about which order to play the two turns in – it's often best to save the best to last and take the lower scoring move first, particularly if it stymies your opponent.

(d) If possible, set up a big scoring final move with your penultimate turn, especially if your opponent can't block it – even if they can, they may have to sacrifice vital points to do so.

(e) Bear in mind your penultimate move is really the most important of the whole game since it's the only one in which you can decide your next turn as well.

(f) In close games, the endgame is all-important. It's amazing how many wins you can eke out from a seemingly forlorn position – never give up.

This, I believe, is the most important Scrabble Secret of all….'The player who wins is the one who truly believes they can – and keeps that belief a secret.'

Two- and Three-Letter Words
Playable in Scrabble

The Two-Letter Words Playable in Scrabble are ...

AA *noun* volcanic rock

AB *noun* abdominal muscle

AD *noun* advertisement

AE *determiner* one

AG *noun* agriculture

AH *interjection* expressing surprise, joy; *verb* say 'ah'

AI *noun* shaggy-coated slow-moving animal of South America

AL *noun* Asian shrub or tree

AM form of the present tense of *be*

AN *determiner* form of *a* used before vowels; *noun* additional condition

AR *noun* letter R

AS *adverb* used to indicate amount or extent in comparisons; *noun* ancient Roman unit of weight

AT *noun* Laotian monetary unit

AW variant of *all*

AX same as *axe*

AY *adverb* ever; *noun* expression of agreement

BA	*noun* symbol for the soul in ancient Egyptian religion
BE	*verb* exist or live
BI	short for *bisexual*
BO	*interjection* uttered to startle or surprise someone; *noun* fellow, buddy
BY	*preposition* indicating the doer of an action, nearness, movement past, etc.; *noun* pass to the next round (of a competition, etc.)
CH	obsolete form of *I*
DA	*noun* Burmese knife
DE	*preposition* of or from
DI	plural of *deus*
DO	*verb* perform or complete (a deed or action); *noun* party, celebration
EA	*noun* river
ED	*noun* editor
EE	Scots word for *eye* (plural EEN)
EF	*noun* letter F
EH	*interjection* exclamation of surprise or inquiry; *verb* say 'eh'
EL	*noun* American elevated railway
EM	*noun* square of a body of any size of type, used as a unit of measurement
EN	*noun* unit of measurement, half the width of an em

ER   *interjection* made when hesitating in speech

ES   *noun* letter S

ET   dialect past tense of *eat*

EW   *interjection* expression of disgust

EX   *preposition* not including; *noun* former husband, wife, etc.; *verb* cross out or delete

FA   *noun* (in tonic sol-fa) fourth degree of any major scale

FE   variant of Hebrew letter *pe*, transliterated as *f*

FY   *interjection* exclamation of disapproval

GI   *noun* white suit worn in martial arts

GO   *verb* move to or from a place; *noun* attempt

GU   *noun* type of violin used in Shetland

HA   *interjection* exclamation of triumph, surprise, or scorn

HE   *pronoun* male person or animal; *noun* male person or animal; *interjection* expression of amusement or derision

HI   *interjection* hello

HM   *interjection* sound made to express hesitation or doubt

HO   *noun* cry of 'ho'; *interjection* imitation or representation of the sound of a deep laugh; *verb* halt

ID   *noun* mind's instinctive unconscious energies

IF	*noun* uncertainty or doubt
IN	*preposition* indicating position inside, state or situation, etc.; *adverb* indicating position inside, entry into, etc.; *adjective* fashionable; *noun* way of approaching or befriending a person; *verb* take in
IO	*interjection* exclamation of triumph; *noun* cry of 'io'
IS	form of the present tense of *be*
IT	*pronoun* refers to a nonhuman, animal, plant, or inanimate object; *noun* player whose turn it is to catch the others in children's games
JA	*interjection and sentence substitute* yes
JO	Scots word for *sweetheart* (plural JOES)
KA	*noun* (in ancient Egypt) type of spirit; *verb* (in archaic usage) help
KI	*noun* vital energy
KO	*noun* (in New Zealand) traditional digging tool
KY	Scots word for *cows*
LA	*noun* the sixth note of the musical scale
LI	*noun* Chinese measurement of distance
LO	*interjection* look!
MA	*noun* mother

ME	*noun* (in tonic sol-fa) third degree of any major scale; *pronoun* refers to the speaker or writer
MI	*noun* (in tonic sol-fa) third degree of any major scale
MM	*interjection* expressing enjoyment of taste or smell
MO	*noun* moment
MU	*noun* twelfth letter in the Greek alphabet
MY	*adjective* belonging to me; *interjection* exclamation of surprise or awe
NA	Scots word for *no*
NE	*conjunction* nor
NO	*interjection* expressing denial, disagreement, or refusal; *adjective* not any, not a; *noun* answer or vote of 'no'
NU	*noun* thirteenth letter in the Greek alphabet
NY	nigh: *preposition* near; *adverb* nearly; *verb* approach
OB	*noun* expression of opposition
OD	*noun* hypothetical force
OE	*noun* grandchild
OF	*preposition* belonging to
OH	*interjection* exclamation of surprise, pain, etc.; *verb* say 'oh'

OI	*interjection* shout to attract attention; *noun* grey-faced petrel
OK	*interjection* expression of approval
OM	*noun* sacred syllable in Hinduism
ON	*preposition* indicating position above, attachment, closeness, etc.; *adjective/adverb* in operation; *noun* side of the field on which the batsman stands (in cricket); *verb* go on
OO	Scots word for *wool*
OP	*noun* operation
OR	*preposition* before; *adjective* of the metal gold; *noun* gold
OS	*noun* mouth or mouthlike part or opening
OU	*interjection* expressing concession; *noun* man, bloke, or chap
OW	*interjection* exclamation of pain
OX	*noun* castrated bull
OY	*noun* grandchild
PA	*noun* (formerly) fortified Māori settlement
PE	*noun* seventeenth letter of the Hebrew alphabet, transliterated as *p*
PI	*noun* sixteenth letter in the Greek alphabet; *verb* spill and mix (set type) indiscriminately
PO	*noun* chamberpot

QI *noun* vital force

RE *preposition* concerning; *noun* the second note of the musical scale

SH *interjection* hush

SI *noun* (in tonic sol-fa) seventh degree of any major scale

SO *adverb* to such an extent; *interjection* exclamation of surprise, triumph, or realization; *noun* the fifth note of the musical scale

ST *interjection* exclamation to attract attention

TA *interjection* thank you

TE *noun* (in tonic sol-fa) seventh degree of any major scale

TI *noun* (in tonic sol-fa) seventh degree of any major scale

TO *preposition* indicating movement towards, equality, or comparison, etc.; *adverb* a closed position

UG *verb* hate

UH *interjection* used to express hesitation

UM *interjection* sound made when hesitating in speech; *verb* hesitate while speaking

UN *pronoun* spelling of *one* to reflect dialectal or informal pronunciation

UP	*adverb* indicating movement to or position at a higher place; *adjective* of a high or higher position; *verb* increase or raise
UR	*interjection* hesitant utterance used to fill gaps in talking
US	*pronoun* refers to the speaker or writer and another person or other people
UT	*noun* syllable used in the fixed system of solmization for the note C
WE	*pronoun* speaker or writer and one or more others
WO	archaic spelling of *woe*
XI	*noun* fourteenth letter in the Greek alphabet
XU	*noun* Vietnamese currency unit
YA	*noun* type of Asian pear
YE	*pronoun* you; *determiner* the
YO	*interjection* used as a greeting
YU	*noun* jade
ZA	*noun* pizza
ZE	*pronoun* gender-neutral pronoun
ZO	*noun* Tibetan breed of cattle

The Three-Letter Words Playable in Scrabble are ...

AAH *verb* exclaim in pleasure

AAL *noun* Asian shrub or tree

AAS inflected form of *aa*

ABA *noun* type of Syrian cloth

ABB *noun* yarn used in weaving

ABS inflected form of *ab*

ABY *verb* pay the penalty for

ACE *noun* playing card with one symbol on it; *adjective* excellent; *verb* serve an ace in racquet sports

ACH *interjection* Scots expression of surprise

ACT *noun* thing done; *verb* do something

ADD *verb* combine (numbers or quantities)

ADO *noun* fuss, trouble

ADS inflected form of *ad*

ADZ *noun* (US) woodworking tool; *verb* use an adz

AFF same as *off*

AFT *adjective/adverb* at or towards the rear of a ship or aircraft

AGA *noun* title of respect

AGE *noun* length of time a person or thing has existed; *verb* make or grow old

AGO   *adverb* in the past

AGS   inflected form of *ag*

AHA   *interjection* exclamation of triumph or surprise

AHI   *noun* yellowfin tuna

AHS   inflected form of *ah*

AIA   *noun* female servant in East Asia

AID   *noun* (give) assistance or support; *verb* help financially or in other ways

AIL   *verb* trouble, afflict

AIM   *verb* point (a weapon or missile) or direct (a blow or remark) at a target; *noun* aiming

AIN   *noun* sixteenth letter in the Hebrew alphabet

AIR   *noun* mixture of gases forming the earth's atmosphere; *verb* make known publicly

AIS   inflected form of *ai*

AIT   *noun* islet, esp in a river

AJI   *noun* type of spicy pepper

AKA   *noun* type of New Zealand vine

AKE   *verb* old spelling of ache

ALA   *noun* winglike structure

ALB   *noun* long white robe worn by a Christian priest

ALE   *noun* kind of beer

ALF   *noun* uncultivated Australian

ALL   *adjective* whole quantity or number (of); *adverb* wholly, entirely; *noun* entire being, effort, or property

ALP   *noun* high mountain

ALS   inflected form of *al*

ALT   *noun* octave directly above the treble staff

ALU   *noun* (in Indian cookery) potato

AMA   *noun* vessel for water

AME   *noun* soul

AMI   *noun* male friend

AMP   *noun* ampere; *verb* excite or become excited

AMU   *noun* unit of mass

ANA   *adverb* in equal quantities; *noun* collection of reminiscences

AND   *noun* additional matter or problem

ANE   Scots word for *one*

ANI   *noun* tropical bird

ANN   *noun* old Scots word for a widow's pension

ANS   *plural noun* as in *ifs and ans* things that might have happened, but which did not

ANT   *noun* small insect living in highly-organized colonies

ANY   *adjective* one or some, no matter which; *adverb* at all

APE *noun* tailless monkey such as the chimpanzee or gorilla; *verb* imitate

APO *noun* type of protein

APP *noun* application program

APT *adjective* having a specified tendency; *verb* be fitting

ARB *noun* arbitrage: purchase of currencies, securities, or commodities in one market for immediate resale in others in order to profit from unequal prices

ARC *noun* part of a circle or other curve; *verb* form an arc

ARD *noun* primitive plough

ARE *noun* unit of measure, 100 square metres; *verb* form of the present tense of be

ARF *noun* barking sound

ARK *noun* boat built by Noah, which survived the Flood; *verb* place in an ark

ARM *noun* limbs from the shoulder to the wrist; *verb* supply with weapons

ARS inflected form of *ar*

ART *noun* creation of works of beauty, esp paintings or sculpture

ARY dialect form of *any*

ASH *noun* powdery substance left when something is burnt; *verb* reduce to ashes

ASK *verb* say (something) in a form that requires an answer

ASP *noun* small poisonous snake

ASS *noun* donkey

ATE past tense of *eat*

ATS inflected form of *at*

ATT *noun* old Siamese coin

AUA *noun* yellow-eye mullet

AUE *interjection* Māori exclamation

AUF old word for *oaf*

AUK *noun* sea bird with short wings

AVA *adverb* at all; *noun* Polynesian shrub

AVE *noun* expression of welcome or farewell

AVO *noun* Macao currency unit

AWA same as *away*

AWE *noun* wonder and respect mixed with dread; *verb* fill with awe

AWK *noun* type of programming language

AWL *noun* pointed tool for piercing wood, leather, etc.

AWN *noun* bristles on grasses

AXE *noun* tool with a sharp blade for felling trees or chopping wood; *verb* dismiss (employees), restrict (expenditure), or terminate (a project)

AYE *noun* affirmative vote or voter; *adverb* always

AYS inflected form of *ay*

AYU   *noun* small Japanese fish

AZO   *adjective* of the divalent group -N:N-

BAA   *verb* the characteristic bleating sound of a sheep; *noun* cry made by a sheep

BAE   *noun* sweetheart or lover

BAC   *noun* baccalaureate

BAD   *adjective* not good; *noun* unfortunate or unpleasant events collectively; *adverb* badly

BAG   *noun* flexible container with an opening at one end; *verb* put into a bag

BAH   *interjection* expressing contempt or disgust

BAL   *noun* balmoral: laced walking shoe

BAM   *verb* cheat

BAN   *verb* prohibit or forbid officially; *noun* unit of currency in Romania

BAO   *noun* steamed dumpling

BAP   *noun* large soft bread roll

BAR   *noun* rigid usually straight length of metal, wood, etc., longer than it is wide or thick; *verb* fasten or secure with a bar

BAS   inflected form of *ba*

BAT   *noun* any of various types of club used to hit the ball in certain sports; *verb* strike with or as if with a bat

BAY   *noun* wide semicircular indentation of a shoreline; *verb* howl in deep tones

BED	*noun* piece of furniture on which to sleep; *verb* plant in a bed
BEE	*noun* insect that makes wax and honey
BEG	*verb* solicit (money, food, etc.), esp in the street
BEL	*noun* unit for comparing two power levels or measuring the intensity of a sound
BEN	*noun* mountain peak; *adverb* in; *adjective* inner
BES	*noun* second letter of the Hebrew alphabet, transliterated as *b*
BET	*noun* wager between two parties predicting different outcomes of an event; *verb* predict
BEY	*noun* (in the Ottoman empire) a title given to senior officers, provincial governors, and certain other officials
BEZ	*noun* part of deer's horn
BIB	*verb* drink
BID	*verb* offer (an amount) in attempting to buy something; *noun* offer of a specified amount, as at an auction
BIG	*adjective* of considerable size, height, number, or capacity; *adverb* on a grand scale; *verb* build
BIN	*noun* container for rubbish or for storing grain, coal, etc.; *verb* put in a rubbish bin
BIO	short for *biography*
BIS	*adverb* twice; *sentence substitute* encore! again!
BIT	*noun* small piece, portion, or quantity

BIZ *noun* business

BOA *noun* large nonvenomous snake

BOB *verb* move or cause to move up and down repeatedly; *noun* short abrupt movement, as of the head

BOD *noun* person

BOG *noun* wet spongy ground; *verb* mire or delay

BOH same as *bo*

BOI *noun* lesbian who dresses like a boy

BOK *noun* South African antelope

BON *adjective* good

BOO *interjection* shout of disapproval; *verb* shout 'boo' to show disapproval

BOP *verb* dance to pop music; *noun* form of jazz with complex rhythms and harmonies

BOR *noun* neighbour

BOS inflected form of *bo*

BOT *verb* scrounge

BOW *verb* lower (one's head) or bend (one's knee or body) as a sign of respect or shame; *noun* movement made when bowing

BOX *noun* container with a firm flat base and sides; *verb* put into a box

BOY *noun* male child; *verb* act the part of a boy in a play

BRA *noun* woman's undergarment

BRO	*noun* family member
BRR	*interjection* used to suggest shivering
BRU	South African word for *friend*
BUB	*noun* youngster
BUD	*noun* swelling on a plant that develops into a leaf or flower; *verb* produce buds
BUG	*noun* insect; *verb* irritate
BUM	*noun* loafer or idler; *verb* get by begging; *adjective* of poor quality
BUN	*noun* small sweet bread roll or cake
BUR	*noun* small rotary file; *verb* form a rough edge on (a workpiece)
BUS	*noun* large motor vehicle for carrying passengers between stops; *verb* travel by bus
BUT	*preposition* except; *adverb* only; *noun* outer room of a two-roomed cottage: usually the kitchen
BUY	*verb* acquire by paying money for; *noun* thing acquired through payment
BYE	*noun* situation where a player or team wins a round by having no opponent; *interjection* goodbye
BYS	inflected form of *by*
CAA	Scots word for *call*
CAB	*noun* taxi; *verb* take a taxi
CAD	*noun* dishonourable man
CAF	short for *cafeteria*

CAG	*noun* cagoule: lightweight hooded waterproof jacket
CAL	short for *calorie*
CAM	*noun* device that converts a circular motion to a to-and-fro motion; *verb* furnish (a machine) with a cam
CAN	*verb* be able to; *noun* metal container for food or liquids
CAP	*noun* soft close-fitting covering for the head; *verb* cover or top with something
CAR	*noun* motor vehicle designed to carry a small number of people
CAT	*noun* small domesticated furry mammal; *verb* flog with a cat-'o-nine-tails
CAW	*noun* cry of a crow, rook, or raven; *verb* make this cry
CAY	*noun* low island or bank composed of sand and coral fragments
CAZ	short for *casual*
CEE	*noun* third letter of the alphabet
CEL	short for *celluloid*
CEP	*noun* edible woodland fungus
CHA	*noun* tea
CHE	dialectal form of *I*
CHI	*noun* twenty-second letter of the Greek alphabet

CID *noun* leader

CIG same as *cigarette*

CIS *adjective* having two groups of atoms on the same side of a double bond

CIT *noun* pejorative term for a town dweller

CLY *verb* steal or seize

COB *noun* stalk of an ear of maize; *verb* beat

COD *noun* large food fish of the North Atlantic; *adjective* having the character of an imitation or parody; *verb* make fun of

COG *noun* one of the teeth on the rim of a gearwheel; *verb* roll (cast-steel ingots) to convert them into blooms

COL *noun* high mountain pass

CON *verb* deceive, swindle; *noun* convict; *preposition* with

COO *verb* (of a dove or pigeon) make a soft murmuring sound; *noun* sound of cooing; *interjection* exclamation of surprise, awe, etc.

COP same as *copper*

COR *interjection* exclamation of surprise, amazement, or admiration

COS *noun* cosine: trigonometric function

COT *noun* baby's bed with high sides; *verb* entangle or become entangled

COW *noun* mature female of certain mammals; *verb* intimidate, subdue

COX *noun* coxswain; *verb* act as cox of (a boat)

COY *adjective* affectedly shy or modest; *verb* caress

COZ archaic word for *cousin*

CRU *noun* (in France) a vineyard, group of vineyards, or wine-producing region

CRY *verb* shed tears; *noun* fit of weeping

CUB *noun* young wild animal such as a bear or fox; *adjective* young or inexperienced; *verb* give birth to cubs

CUD *noun* partially digested food chewed by a ruminant

CUE *noun* signal to an actor or musician to begin speaking or playing; *verb* give a cue to

CUM *preposition* with

CUP *noun* small bowl-shaped drinking container with a handle; *verb* form (one's hands) into the shape of a cup

CUR *noun* mongrel dog

CUT *verb* open up, penetrate, wound, or divide with a sharp instrument

CUZ *noun* cousin

CWM *noun* steep-sided semicircular hollow found in mountainous areas

DAB *verb* pat lightly; *noun* small amount of something soft or moist

DAD *noun* father; *verb* act or treat as a father

DAE Scots word for *do*

DAG *noun* character; *verb* cut daglocks from sheep

DAH *noun* long sound used in Morse code

DAK *noun* system of mail delivery or passenger transport

DAL *noun* decalitre

DAM *noun* barrier built across a river to create a lake; *verb* build a dam across (a river)

DAN *noun* in judo, any of the ten black-belt grades of proficiency

DAP *verb* engage in a type of fly fishing

DAS inflected form of *da*

DAW *noun* archaic, dialect, or poetic name for a jackdaw; *verb* old word for dawn

DAY *noun* period of 24 hours

DEB *noun* debutante

DEE Scots word for *die*

DEF *adjective* very good

DEG *verb* water (a plant, etc.)

DEI plural of *deus*

DEL *noun* differential operator

DEN *noun* home of a wild animal; *verb* live in or as if in a den

DEP   *noun* small shop where newspapers, sweets, soft drinks, etc. are sold

DEV   *noun* deva: (in Hinduism and Buddhism) divine being or god

DEW   *noun* drops of water that form on the ground at night from vapour in the air; *verb* moisten with or as with dew

DEX   *noun* dextroamphetamine

DEY   *noun* title given to commanders or governors of the Janissaries of Algiers

DIB   *verb* fish by allowing the bait to bob and dip on the surface

DID   inflected form of *do*

DIE   *verb* cease all biological activity permanently; *noun* shaped block used to cut or form metal

DIF   *noun* (slang) difference

DIG   *verb* cut into, break up, and turn over or remove (earth), esp with a spade; *noun* digging

DIM   *adjective* badly lit; *verb* make or become dim

DIN   *noun* loud unpleasant confused noise; *verb* instil (something) into someone by constant repetition

DIP   *verb* plunge quickly or briefly into a liquid; *noun* dipping

DIS   *verb* treat (a person) with contempt

DIT   *verb* stop something happening; *noun* short sound used in the spoken representation of telegraphic codes

DIV   *noun* stupid or foolish person

DOB   *verb* as in *dob in* inform against or report

DOC   same as *doctor*

DOD   *verb* clip

DOE   *noun* female deer, hare, or rabbit

DOF   informal South African word for *stupid*

DOG   *noun* domesticated four-legged mammal; *verb* follow (someone) closely

DOH   *noun* (in tonic sol-fa) first degree of any major scale; *interjection* exclamation of annoyance when something goes wrong

DOL   *noun* unit of pain intensity, as measured by dolorimetry

DOM   *noun* title given to various monks and to certain of the canons regular

DON   *verb* put on (clothing); *noun* member of the teaching staff at a university or college

DOO   Scots word for *dove*

DOP   *verb* curtsy; *noun* tot or small drink, usually alcoholic; *verb* fail to reach the required standard in (an examination, course, etc.)

DOR   *noun* European dung beetle; *verb* mock

DOS   inflected form of *do*

DOT *noun* small round mark; *verb* mark with a dot

DOW *verb* archaic word meaning to be of worth

DOX *verb* publish someone's personal information on the internet

DOY *noun* beloved person: used esp as an endearment

DRY *adjective* lacking moisture; *verb* make or become dry

DSO same as *zo*

DUB *verb* give (a person or place) a name or nickname; *noun* style of reggae record production

DUD *noun* ineffectual person or thing; *adjective* bad or useless

DUE *verb* supply with; *adjective* expected or scheduled to be present or arrive; *noun* something that is owed or required; *adverb* directly or exactly

DUG Scots word for *dog*

DUH *interjection* ironic response to a question or statement

DUI inflected form of *duo*

DUM *adjective* steamed

DUN *adjective* brownish-grey; *verb* demand payment from (a debtor); *noun* demand for payment

DUO same as *duet*

DUP *verb* open

DUX *noun* (in Scottish and certain other schools) the top pupil in a class or school

DYE *noun* colouring substance; *verb* colour (hair or fabric) by applying a dye

DZO variant spelling of *zo*

EAN *verb* give birth

EAR *noun* organ of hearing, esp the external part of it; *verb* (of cereal plants) to develop parts that contain seeds, grains, or kernels

EAS inflected form of *ea*

EAT *verb* take (food) into the mouth and swallow it

EAU same as *ea*

EBB *verb* (of tide water) flow back; *noun* flowing back of the tide

ECH *verb* eke out

ECO *noun* ecology activist

ECU *noun* any of various former French gold or silver coins

EDH *noun* character of the runic alphabet

EDS inflected form of *ed*

EEK *interjection* indicating shock or fright

EEL *noun* snakelike fish

EEN inflected form of *ee*

EEW	*interjection*	exclamation of disgust

EEW *interjection* exclamation of disgust

EFF *verb* use bad language

EFS inflected form of *ef*

EFT *noun* dialect or archaic name for a newt; *adverb* again

EGG *noun* object laid by birds and other creatures, containing a developing embryo; *verb* urge or incite, esp to daring or foolish acts

EGO *noun* conscious mind of an individual

EHS inflected form of *eh*

EIK variant form of *eke*

EKE *verb* increase, enlarge, or lengthen

ELD *noun* old age

ELF *noun* (in folklore) small mischievous fairy; *verb* entangle (esp hair)

ELK *noun* large deer of North Europe and Asia

ELL *noun* obsolete unit of length

ELM *noun* tree with serrated leaves

ELS inflected form of *el*

ELT *noun* young female pig

EME *noun* uncle

EMO *noun* type of music

EMS inflected form of *em*

EMU *noun* large Australian flightless bird with long legs

END *noun* furthest point or part; *verb* bring or come to a finish

ENE variant of *even*

ENG *noun* symbol used to represent a velar nasal consonant

ENS *noun* being or existence in the most general abstract sense

EON *noun* two or more eras

ERA *noun* period of time considered as distinctive

ERE *preposition* before; *verb* plough

ERF *noun* plot of land marked off for building purposes

ERG *noun* ergometer: instrument measuring power or force

ERK *noun* aircraftman or naval rating

ERM *interjection* expressing hesitation

ERN archaic variant of *earn*

ERR *verb* make a mistake

ERS *noun* type of vetch (leguminous climbing plant)

ESS *noun* letter S

EST *noun* treatment intended to help people towards psychological growth

ETA *noun* seventh letter in the Greek alphabet

ETH same as *edh*

EUK *verb* itch

EVE *noun* evening or day before some special event

EVO informal word for *evening*

EWE *noun* female sheep

EWK *verb* itch

EWT archaic form of *newt*

EXO informal word for *excellent*

EYE *noun* organ of sight; *verb* look at carefully or warily

FAA Scots word for *fall*

FAB *adjective* excellent; *noun* fabrication

FAD *noun* short-lived fashion

FAE Scots word for *from*

FAG *noun* boring or wearisome task; *verb* become exhausted by work

FAH *noun* (in tonic sol-fa) fourth degree of any major scale

FAN *noun* object used to create a current of air; *verb* blow or cool with a fan

FAP *adjective* drunk

FAR *adverb* at, to, or from a great distance; *adjective* remote in space or time; *verb* go far

FAS inflected form of *fa*

FAT *adjective* having excess flesh on the body; *noun* extra flesh on the body; *verb* fatten

FAW	*noun* gypsy
FAX	*noun* electronic system; *verb* send (a document) by this system
FAY	*noun* fairy or sprite; *adjective* of or resembling a fay; *verb* fit or be fitted closely or tightly
FED	*noun* FBI agent
FEE	*noun* charge paid to be allowed to do something; *verb* pay a fee to
FEG	same as *fig*
FEH	same as *fe*
FEM	*noun* type of igneous rock
FEN	*noun* low-lying flat marshy land
FER	same as *far*
FES	inflected form of *fe*
FET	*verb* fetch
FEU	*noun* (in Scotland) type of rent; *verb* grant land to a person who pays a feu
FEW	*adjective* not many; *noun* as in the few small number of people considered as a class
FEY	*adjective* whimsically strange; *verb* clean out
FEZ	*noun* brimless tasselled cap, originally from Turkey
FIB	*noun* trivial lie; *verb* tell a lie
FID	*noun* spike for separating strands of rope in splicing

FIE	same as *fey*
FIG	*noun* soft pear-shaped fruit; *verb* dress (up) or rig (out)
FIL	*noun* monetary unit of Bahrain, Iraq, Jordan, and Kuwait
FIN	*noun* any of the appendages of some aquatic animals; *verb* provide with fins
FIR	*noun* pyramid-shaped tree
FIT	*verb* be appropriate or suitable for; *adjective* appropriate; *noun* way in which something fits
FIX	*verb* make or become firm, stable, or secure; *noun* difficult situation
FIZ	same as *fizz*
FLU	*noun* any of various viral infections
FLY	*verb* move through the air on wings or in an aircraft; *noun* fastening at the front of trousers; *adjective* sharp and cunning
FOB	*noun* short watch chain; *verb* cheat
FOE	*noun* enemy, opponent
FOG	*noun* mass of condensed water vapour in the lower air; *verb* cover with steam
FOH	*interjection* expressing disgust
FON	*verb* compel
FOO	*noun* temporary computer variable or file

FOP *noun* man excessively concerned with fashion; *verb* act like a fop

FOR *preposition* indicating a person intended to benefit from or receive something, span of time or distance, person or thing represented by someone, etc.

FOU *adjective* full; *noun* bushel

FOX *noun* reddish-brown bushy-tailed animal of the dog family; *verb* perplex or deceive

FOY *noun* loyalty

FRA *noun* brother: a title given to an Italian monk or friar

FRO *adverb* away; *noun* afro

FRY *verb* cook or be cooked in fat or oil; *noun* dish of fried food

FUB *verb* cheat

FUD *noun* rabbit's tail

FUG *noun* hot stale atmosphere; *verb* sit in a fug

FUM *noun* phoenix, in Chinese mythology

FUN *noun* enjoyment or amusement; *verb* trick

FUR *noun* soft hair of a mammal; *verb* cover or become covered with fur

GAB *verb* talk or chatter; *noun* mechanical device

GAD *verb* go about in search of pleasure; *noun* carefree adventure

GAE Scots word for *go*

GAG   *verb* choke or retch; *noun* cloth etc. put into or tied across the mouth

GAK   *noun* slang word for cocaine

GAL   *noun* girl

GAM   *noun* school of whales; *verb* (of whales) form a school

GAN   *verb* go

GAP   *noun* break or opening

GAR   *noun* primitive freshwater bony fish

GAS   *noun* airlike substance that is not liquid or solid; *verb* poison or render unconscious with gas

GAT   *noun* pistol or revolver

GAU   *noun* district set up by the Nazi Party

GAW   *noun* as in *weather gaw* partial rainbow

GAY   *adjective* homosexual; *noun* homosexual

GED   *noun* (Scots) pike: large predatory freshwater fish

GEE   *interjection* mild exclamation of surprise, admiration, etc.; *verb* move (an animal, esp a horse) ahead

GEL   *noun* jelly-like substance; *verb* form a gel

GEM   *noun* precious stone or jewel; *verb* set or ornament with gems

GEN   *noun* information; *verb* gain information

GEO   *noun* (esp in Shetland) a small fjord or gully

GER *noun* portable Mongolian dwelling

GET *verb* obtain or receive

GEY *adverb* extremely; *adjective* gallant

GHI *noun* (in Indian cookery) clarified butter

GIB *noun* metal wedge, pad, or thrust bearing; *verb* fasten or supply with a gib

GID *noun* disease of sheep

GIE Scots word for *give*

GIF *noun* file held in GIF format (a compressed format for a series of pictures)

GIG *noun* single performance by pop or jazz musicians; *verb* play a gig or gigs

GIN *noun* spirit flavoured with juniper berries; *verb* free (cotton) of seeds with an engine; begin

GIO same as *geo*

GIP same as *gyp*

GIS inflected form of *gi*

GIT *noun* contemptible person; *verb* dialect version of get

GJU *noun* type of violin used in Shetland

GNU *noun* ox-like South African antelope

GOA *noun* Tibetan gazelle

GOB *noun* lump of a soft substance; *verb* spit

GOD *noun* spirit or being worshipped as having supernatural power; *verb* deify

GOE	same as *go*
GON	*noun* geometrical grade
GOO	*noun* sticky substance
GOR	*interjection* God!; *noun* seagull
GOS	inflected form of *go*
GOT	inflected form of *get*
GOV	*noun* boss
GOX	*noun* gaseous oxygen
GRR	*interjection* expressing anger or annoyance
GUB	*noun* Scots word for mouth; *verb* hit or defeat
GUE	same as *gju*
GUL	*noun* design used in Turkoman carpets
GUM	*noun* any of various sticky substances; *verb* stick with gum
GUN	*noun* weapon with a tube from which missiles are fired; *verb* cause (an engine) to run at high speed
GUP	*noun* gossip
GUR	*noun* unrefined cane sugar
GUS	inflected form of *gu*
GUT	*noun* intestine; *verb* remove the guts from; *adjective* basic or instinctive
GUV	informal name for *governor*
GUY	*noun* man or boy; *verb* make fun of

GYM   *noun* gymnasium

GYP   *noun* slang word for severe pain

HAD   Scots form of to hold

HAE   Scots variant of *have*

HAG   *noun* ugly old woman; *verb* hack

HAH   same as *ha*

HAJ   *noun* pilgrimage a Muslim makes to Mecca

HAM   *noun* smoked or salted meat from a pig's thigh; *verb* overact

HAN   archaic inflected form of *have*

HAO   *noun* monetary unit of Vietnam

HAP   *noun* luck; *verb* cover up

HAS   form of the present tense of *have*

HAT   *noun* covering for the head, often with a brim; *verb* supply (a person) with a hat or put a hat on (someone)

HAW   *noun* hawthorn berry; *verb* make an inarticulate utterance

HAY   *noun* grass cut and dried as fodder; *verb* cut, dry, and store (grass, clover, etc.) as fodder

HEH   *interjection* exclamation of surprise or inquiry

HEM   *noun* bottom edge of a garment; *verb* provide with a hem

HEN   *noun* female domestic fowl; *verb* lose one's courage

HEP *adjective* aware of or following the latest trends

HER *pronoun* refers to anything personified as feminine; *adjective* belonging to her; *determiner* of, belonging to, or associated with her

HES inflected form of *he*

HET *noun* short for heterosexual; *adjective* Scots word for hot

HEW *verb* cut with an axe

HEX *adjective* of or relating to hexadecimal notation; *noun* evil spell; *verb* bewitch

HEY *interjection* expressing surprise or for catching attention; *verb* perform a country dance

HIC representation of the sound of a hiccup

HID inflected form of *hide*

HIE *verb* hurry

HIM *pronoun* refers to a male person or animal; *noun* male person

HIN *noun* Hebrew unit of capacity

HIP *noun* either side of the body between the pelvis and the thigh; *adjective* aware of or following the latest trends; *interjection* exclamation used to introduce cheers

HIS *adjective* belonging to him

HIT *verb* strike, touch forcefully; *noun* hitting

HMM same as *hm*

HOA same as *ho*

HOB *noun* flat top part of a cooker; *verb* cut or form with a hob

HOC *adjective* Latin for this

HOD *noun* open wooden box attached to a pole; *verb* bob up and down

HOE *noun* long-handled tool used for loosening soil or weeding; *verb* scrape or weed with a hoe

HOG *noun* castrated male pig; *verb* take more than one's share of

HOH same as *ho*

HOI same as *hoy*

HOM *noun* sacred plant of the Parsees and ancient Persians

HON short for *honey*

HOO *interjection* expressing joy, excitement, etc.

HOP *verb* jump on one foot; *noun* instance of hopping

HOS inflected form of *ho*

HOT *adjective* having a high temperature

HOW *adverb* in what way, by what means; *noun* the way a thing is done; *sentence substitute* supposed Native American greeting

HOX *verb* hamstring

HOY *interjection* cry used to attract someone's attention; *noun* freight barge; *verb* drive animal with cry

HUB *noun* centre of a wheel, through which the axle passes

HUE *noun* colour, shade

HUG *verb* clasp tightly in the arms, usually with affection; *noun* tight or fond embrace

HUH *interjection* exclamation of derision or inquiry

HUI *noun* meeting of Māori people

HUM *verb* make a low continuous vibrating sound; *noun* humming sound

HUN *noun* member of any of several nomadic peoples

HUP *verb* cry 'hup' to get a horse to move

HUT *noun* small house, shelter, or shed

HYE same as *hie*

HYP short for *hypotenuse*

ICE *noun* water in the solid state, formed by freezing liquid water; *verb* form or cause to form ice

ICH archaic form of *eke*

ICK *interjection* expressing disgust

ICY *adjective* very cold

IDE *noun* silver orfe fish

IDS inflected form of *id*

IFF *conjunction* in logic, a shortened form of 'if and only if'

IFS inflected form of *if*

IGG *verb* antagonize

ILK *noun* type; *determiner* each

ILL *adjective* not in good health; *noun* evil, harm; *adverb* badly

IMP *noun* (in folklore) creature with magical powers; *verb* method of repairing the wing of a hawk or falcon

ING *noun* meadow near a river

INK *noun* coloured liquid used for writing or printing; *verb* mark in ink (something already marked in pencil)

INN *noun* pub or small hotel, esp in the country; *verb* stay at an inn

INS inflected form of *in*

ION *noun* electrically charged atom

IOS inflected form of *io*

IRE *verb* anger; *noun* anger

IRK *verb* irritate, annoy

ISH *noun* issue

ISM *noun* doctrine, system, or practice

ISO	*noun* short segment of film that can be replayed easily
ITA	*noun* type of palm
ITS	*determiner* belonging to it; *adjective* of or belonging to it
IVY	*noun* evergreen climbing plant
IWI	*noun* Māori tribe
JAB	*verb* poke sharply; *noun* quick punch or poke
JAG	*noun* period of uncontrolled indulgence in an activity; *verb* cut unevenly
JAI	*interjection* victory (to)
JAK	same as *jack*
JAM	*verb* pack tightly into a place; *noun* fruit preserve; hold-up of traffic
JAP	*verb* splash
JAR	*noun* wide-mouthed container; *verb* have a disturbing or unpleasant effect
JAW	*noun* one of the bones in which the teeth are set; *verb* talk lengthily
JAY	*noun* type of bird
JEE	variant of *gee*
JET	*noun* aircraft driven by jet propulsion; *verb* fly by jet aircraft
JEU	*noun* game

JIB same as *jibe*

JIG *noun* type of lively dance; *verb* dance a jig

JIN *noun* Chinese unit of weight

JIZ *noun* wig

JOB *noun* occupation or paid employment; *verb* work at casual jobs

JOE same as *jo*

JOG *verb* run at a gentle pace, esp for exercise; *noun* slow run

JOL *noun* party; *verb* have a good time

JOR *noun* movement in Indian music

JOT *verb* write briefly; *noun* very small amount

JOW *verb* ring (a bell)

JOY *noun* feeling of great delight or pleasure; *verb* feel joy

JUD *noun* large block of coal

JUG *noun* container for liquids; *verb* stew or boil (meat, esp hare) in an earthenware container

JUN *noun* North and South Korean monetary unit

JUS *noun* right, power, or authority

JUT *verb* project or stick out; *noun* something that juts out

KAB variant spelling of *cab*

KAE *noun* dialect word for jackdaw or jay; *verb* (in archaic usage) help

172

KAF *noun* letter of the Hebrew alphabet

KAI *noun* food

KAK vulgar South African slang word for *faeces*

KAM Shakespearean word for *crooked*

KAS inflected form of *ka*

KAT *noun* white-flowered evergreen shrub

KAW variant spelling of *caw*

KAY *noun* name of the letter K

KEA *noun* large brownish-green parrot of New Zealand

KEB *verb* Scots word meaning to miscarry or reject a lamb

KED *noun* as in *sheep ked* sheep tick

KEF same as *kif*

KEG *noun* small metal beer barrel; *verb* put in kegs

KEN *verb* know; *noun* range of knowledge or perception

KEP *verb* catch

KET dialect word for *carrion*

KEX *noun* any of several hollow-stemmed umbelliferous plants

KEY *noun* device for operating a lock by moving a bolt; *adjective* of great importance; *verb* enter (text) using a keyboard

KHI same as *chi*

KID *noun* child; *verb* tease or deceive (someone); *adjective* younger

KIF *noun* type of drug

KIN *noun* person's relatives collectively; *adjective* related by blood

KIP *verb* sleep; *noun* sleep or slumber

KIR *noun* drink made from dry white wine and cassis

KIS inflected form of *ki*

KIT *noun* outfit or equipment for a specific purpose; *verb* fit or provide

KOA *noun* Hawaiian leguminous tree

KOB *noun* any of several species of antelope

KOI *noun* any of various ornamental forms of the common carp

KON old word for *know*

KOP *noun* prominent isolated hill or mountain in southern Africa

KOR *noun* ancient Hebrew unit of capacity

KOS *noun* Indian unit of distance

KOW old variant of *cow*

KUE *noun* name of the letter Q

KYE *noun* Korean fundraising meeting

KYU *noun* (in judo) one of the five student grades

LAB *noun* laboratory

LAC *noun* (in India) 100,000, esp referring to this sum of rupees

LAD *noun* boy or young man

LAG *verb* go too slowly, fall behind; *noun* delay between events

LAH *noun* (in tonic sol-fa) sixth degree of any major scale

LAM *verb* attack vigorously

LAP *noun* part between the waist and knees when sitting; *verb* overtake so as to be one or more circuits ahead

LAR *noun* boy or young man

LAS inflected form of *la*

LAT *noun* former coin of Latvia

LAV short for *lavatory*

LAW *noun* rule binding on a community; *verb* prosecute; *adjective* (in archaic usage) low

LAX *adjective* not strict; *noun* laxative

LAY inflected form of *lie*

LEA *noun* meadow

LED inflected form of *lead*

LEE *noun* sheltered side; *verb* Scots form of lie

LEG *noun* limb on which a person or animal walks, runs, or stands

LEI inflected form of *leu*

LEK   *noun* bird display area; *verb* gather at lek

LEP   dialect word for *leap*

LET   *noun* act of letting property; *verb* obstruct

LEU   *noun* monetary unit of Romania

LEV   *noun* monetary unit of Bulgaria

LEW   *adjective* tepid

LEX   *noun* system or body of laws

LEY   *noun* land under grass

LIB   *noun* informal word for liberation; *verb* geld

LID   *noun* movable cover

LIE   *verb* make a false statement; *noun* falsehood

LIG   *noun* function with free entertainment and refreshments; *verb* attend such a function

LIN   *verb* cease

LIP   *noun* either of the fleshy edges of the mouth; *verb* touch with the lips

LIS   *noun* fleur-de-lis

LIT   *noun* (archaic) dye or colouring

LOB   *noun* ball struck in a high arc; *verb* strike in a high arc

LOD   *noun* type of logarithm

LOG   *noun* portion of a felled tree stripped of branches; *verb* saw logs from a tree

LOO   *noun* toilet; *verb* Scots word meaning to love

LOP   *verb* cut away; *noun* part(s) lopped off

LOR	*interjection* exclamation of surprise or dismay
LOS	*noun* approval
LOT	*pronoun* great number; *noun* collection of people or things; *verb* draw lots for
LOU	Scots word for *love*
LOW	*adjective* not high; *adverb* in a low position; *noun* low position; *verb* moo
LOX	*verb* load fuel tanks of spacecraft with liquid oxygen; *noun* kind of smoked salmon
LOY	*noun* narrow spade with a single footrest
LUD	*noun* lord; *interjection* exclamation of dismay or surprise
LUG	*verb* carry with great effort; *noun* projection serving as a handle
LUM	*noun* chimney
LUN	*noun* sheltered spot
LUR	*noun* large bronze musical horn
LUV	*noun* love; *verb* love
LUX	*noun* unit of illumination; *verb* clean with a vacuum cleaner
LUZ	*noun* supposedly indestructible bone of the human body
LYE	*noun* caustic solution
LYM	*noun* lyam: leash

MAA *verb* (of goats) bleat

MAC *noun* macintosh

MAD *adjective* mentally deranged, insane; *verb* make mad

MAE *adjective* more

MAG *verb* talk; *noun* talk

MAK Scots word for *make*

MAL *noun* illness

MAM same as *mother*

MAN *noun* adult male; *verb* supply with sufficient people for operation or defence

MAP *noun* representation of the earth's surface or some part of it; *verb* make a map of

MAR *verb* spoil or impair; *noun* disfiguring mark

MAS inflected form of *ma*

MAT *noun* piece of fabric used as a floor covering or to protect a surface; *verb* tangle or become tangled into a dense mass; *adjective* having a dull, lustreless, or roughened surface

MAW *noun* animal's mouth, throat, or stomach; *verb* eat or bite

MAX *verb* reach the full extent

MAY *verb* used as an auxiliary to express possibility, permission, opportunity, etc.

MED	*noun* doctor	
MEE	*noun* Malaysian noodle dish	
MEG	*noun* megabyte: 1,048,576 bytes	
MEH	expression of indifference or boredom	
MEL	*noun* pure form of honey	
MEM	*noun* thirteenth letter in the Hebrew alphabet, transliterated as *m*	
MEN	inflected form of *man*	
MES	inflected form of *me*	
MET	*noun* meteorology	
MEU	*noun* European umbelliferous plant	
MEW	*noun* cry of a cat; *verb* utter this cry	
MHO	*noun* SI unit of electrical conductance	
MIB	*noun* marble used in games	
MIC	*noun* microphone	
MID	*adjective* intermediate, middle; *noun* middle; *preposition* amid	
MIG	*noun* marble used in games	
MIL	*noun* unit of length equal to one thousandth of an inch	
MIM	*adjective* prim, modest, or demure	
MIR	*noun* peasant commune in prerevolutionary Russia	
MIS	inflected form of *mi*	

MIX	*verb* combine or blend into one mass; *noun* mixture
MIZ	shortened form of *misery*
MMM	*interjection* expressing agreement or enjoyment
MNA	*noun* ancient unit of weight and money, used in Asia Minor
MOA	*noun* large extinct flightless New Zealand bird
MOB	*noun* disorderly crowd; *verb* surround in a mob
MOC	*noun* moccasin: soft leather shoe
MOD	*noun* member of a group of fashionable young people, originally in the 1960s; *verb* modify (a piece of software or hardware)
MOE	*adverb* more; *noun* wry face
MOG	*verb* go away
MOI	*pronoun* (used facetiously) me
MOL	*noun* mole: SI unit of amount of substance
MOM	same as *mother*
MON	dialect variant of *man*
MOO	*noun* long deep cry of a cow; *verb* make this noise; *interjection* instance or imitation of this sound
MOP	*noun* long stick with twists of cotton or a sponge on the end, used for cleaning; *verb* clean or soak up with or as if with a mop
MOR	*noun* layer of acidic humus formed in cool

moist areas

MOS inflected form of *mo*

MOT *noun* girl or young woman, esp one's girlfriend

MOU Scots word for *mouth*

MOW *verb* cut (grass or crops); *noun* part of a barn where hay, straw, etc., is stored

MOY *noun* coin

MOZ *noun* hex

MUD *noun* wet soft earth; *verb* cover in mud

MUG *noun* large drinking cup; *verb* attack in order to rob

MUM *noun* mother; *verb* act in a mummer's play

MUN *verb* maun: dialect word for *must*

MUS inflected form of *mu*

MUT another word for *em*

MUX *verb* spoil

MYC *noun* oncogene that aids the growth of tumorous cells

NAB *verb* arrest (someone)

NAE Scots word for *no*

NAG *verb* scold or find fault constantly; *noun* person who nags

NAH same as *no*

NAM *noun* distraint

NAN *noun* grandmother

NAP *noun* short sleep; *verb* have a short sleep

NAS *verb* has not

NAT *noun* supporter of nationalism

NAV short for *navigation*

NAW same as *no*

NAY *interjection* no; *noun* person who votes against a motion; *adverb* used for emphasis; *sentence substitute* no

NEB *noun* beak of a bird or the nose of an animal; *verb* look around nosily

NED *noun* derogatory name for an adolescent considered to be a hooligan

NEE *adjective/preposition* indicating the maiden name of a married woman

NEF *noun* church nave

NEG *noun* photographic negative

NEK *noun* mountain pass

NEP *noun* catmint

NET *noun* fabric of meshes of string, thread, or wire with many openings; *verb* catch (a fish or animal) in a net; *adjective* left after all deductions

NEW *adjective* not existing before; *adverb* recently; *verb* make new

NIB	*noun* writing point of a pen; *verb* provide with a nib
NID	*verb* nest
NIE	archaic spelling of *nigh*
NIL	*noun* nothing, zero
NIM	*noun* game involving removing one or more small items from several rows or piles; *verb* steal
NIP	*verb* hurry; *noun* pinch or light bite
NIS	*noun* friendly goblin
NIT	*noun* egg or larva of a louse
NIX	*sentence substitute* be careful! watch out!; *noun* rejection or refusal; *verb* veto, deny, reject, or forbid (plans, suggestions, etc.)
NOB	*noun* person of wealth or social distinction
NOD	*verb* lower and raise (one's head) briefly in agreement or greeting; *noun* act of nodding
NOG	*noun* short horizontal timber member
NOH	*noun* stylized classic drama of Japan
NOM	*noun* name
NON	*adverb* not: expressing negation, refusal, or denial
NOO	*noun* type of Japanese musical drama
NOR	*preposition* and not
NOS	inflected form of *no*

NOT   *adverb* expressing negation, refusal, or denial

NOW   *adverb* at or for the present time

NOX   *noun* nitrogen oxide

NOY   *verb* harass

NTH   *adjective* of an unspecified number

NUB   *noun* point or gist (of a story etc.); *verb* hang from the gallows

NUG   *noun* lump of wood sawn from a log

NUN   *noun* female member of a religious order

NUR   *noun* wooden ball

NUS   inflected form of *nu*

NUT   *noun* fruit consisting of a hard shell and a kernel; *verb* gather nuts

NYE   *noun* flock of pheasants; *verb* near

NYM   *adjective* as in *nym war* dispute about publishing material online under a pseudonym

NYS   inflected form of *ny*

OAF   *noun* stupid or clumsy person

OAK   *noun* deciduous forest tree

OAR   *noun* pole with a broad blade, used for rowing a boat; *verb* propel with oars

OAT   *noun* hard cereal grown as food

OBA   *noun* (in West Africa) a Yoruba chief or ruler

OBE   *noun* ancient Laconian village

OBI	*noun* broad sash tied in a large flat bow at the back; *verb* bewitch
OBO	*noun* ship carrying oil and ore
OBS	inflected form of *ob*
OCA	*noun* any of various South American herbaceous plants
OCH	*interjection* expressing surprise, annoyance, or disagreement
ODA	*noun* room in a harem
ODD	*adjective* unusual
ODE	*noun* lyric poem, usually addressed to a particular subject
ODS	inflected form of *od*
OES	inflected form of *oe*
OFF	*preposition* away from; *adverb* away; *adjective* not operating; *noun* side of the field to which the batsman's feet point; *verb* kill
OFT	*adverb* often
OHM	*noun* unit of electrical resistance
OHO	*interjection* exclamation expressing surprise, exultation, or derision
OHS	inflected form of *oh*
OIK	*noun* offensive word for a person regarded as inferior because they are ignorant or lower-class
OIL	*noun* viscous liquid, insoluble in water and

usually flammable; *verb* lubricate (a machine) with oil

OIS   inflected form of *oi*

OKA   *noun* unit of weight used in Turkey

OKE   same as *oka*

OLD   *adjective* having lived or existed for a long time; *noun* earlier or past time

OLE   *interjection* exclamation of approval or encouragement customary at bullfights; *noun* cry of 'olé'

OLM   *noun* pale blind eel-like salamander

OMA   *noun* grandmother

OMS   inflected form of *om*

ONE   *adjective* single, lone; *noun* number or figure 1; *pronoun* any person

ONO   *noun* Hawaiian fish

ONS   inflected form of *on*

ONY   Scots word for *any*

OOF   *noun* money

OOH   *interjection* exclamation of surprise, pleasure, pain, etc.; *verb* say 'ooh'

OOM   *noun* title of respect used to refer to an elderly man

OON   Scots word for *oven*

OOP   *verb* Scots word meaning to bind

OOR	Scots form of *our*
OOS	inflected form of *oo*
OOT	Scots word for *out*
OPA	*noun* grandfather
OPE	archaic or poetic word for *open*
OPS	inflected form of *op*
OPT	*verb* show a preference, choose
ORA	inflected form of *os*
ORB	*noun* ceremonial decorated sphere; *verb* make or become circular or spherical
ORC	*noun* any of various whales, such as the killer and grampus
ORD	*noun* pointed weapon
ORE	*noun* (rock containing) a mineral which yields metal
ORF	*noun* infectious disease of sheep
ORG	*noun* organization
ORS	inflected form of *or*
ORT	*noun* fragment
OSE	*noun* long ridge of gravel, sand, etc.
OUD	*noun* Arabic stringed musical instrument
OUK	Scots word for *week*
OUP	same as *oop*
OUR	*adjective* belonging to us; *determiner* of, belonging to, or associated in some way with us

OUS inflected form of *ou*

OUT *adjective* denoting movement or distance away from; *verb* name (a public figure) as being homosexual

OVA plural of *ovum* (unfertilized egg cell)

OWE *verb* be obliged to pay (a sum of money) to (a person)

OWL *noun* night bird of prey; *verb* act like an owl

OWN *adjective* used to emphasize possession; *pronoun* thing(s) belonging to a particular person; *verb* possess

OWT dialect word for *anything*

OXO *noun* as in *oxo acid* acid that contains oxygen

OXY inflected form of *ox*

OYE same as *oy*

OYS inflected form of *oy*

PAC *noun* soft shoe

PAD *noun* piece of soft material used for protection, support, absorption of liquid, etc.; *verb* protect or fill with soft material

PAH same as *pa*

PAK *noun* pack

PAL *noun* friend; *verb* associate as friends

PAM *noun* knave of clubs

PAN *noun* wide long-handled metal container used in cooking; *verb* sift gravel from (a river) in a pan to search for gold

PAP *noun* soft food for babies or invalids; *verb* (of the paparazzi) follow and photograph (a famous person); feed with pap

PAR *noun* usual or average condition; *verb* play (a golf hole) in par

PAS *noun* dance step or movement, esp in ballet

PAT *verb* tap lightly; *noun* gentle tap or stroke; *adjective* quick, ready, or glib

PAV *noun* pavlova: meringue cake topped with whipped cream and fruit

PAW *noun* animal's foot with claws and pads; *verb* scrape with the paw or hoof

PAX *noun* peace; *interjection* signalling a desire to end hostilities

PAY *verb* give money etc. in return for goods or services; *noun* wages or salary

PEA *noun* climbing plant with seeds growing in pods

PEC *noun* pectoral muscle

PED *noun* pannier

PEE *verb* slang word for *urinate*; *noun* slang word for *urine*

PEG *noun* pin or clip for joining, fastening, marking, etc.; *verb* fasten with pegs

PEH inflected form of *pe*

PEL *noun* pixel

PEN *noun* instrument for writing in ink; *verb* write or compose

PEP *noun* high spirits, energy, or enthusiasm; *verb* liven by imbuing with new vigour

PER *preposition* for each

PES *noun* animal part corresponding to the foot

PET *noun* animal kept for pleasure and companionship; *adjective* kept as a pet; *verb* treat as a pet

PEW *noun* fixed benchlike seat in a church

PHI *noun* twenty-first letter in the Greek alphabet

PHO *noun* Vietnamese noodle soup

PHT *interjection* expressing irritation or reluctance

PIA *noun* innermost of the three membranes that cover the brain and the spinal cord

PIC *noun* photograph or illustration

PIE *noun* dish of meat, fruit, etc. baked in pastry

PIG *noun* animal kept and killed for pork, ham, and bacon; *verb* eat greedily

PIN *noun* short thin piece of stiff wire with a point and head, for fastening things; *verb* fasten with a pin

PIP	*noun* small seed in a fruit; *verb* chirp
PIR	*noun* Sufi master
PIS	inflected form of *pi*
PIT	*noun* deep hole in the ground; *verb* mark with small dents or scars
PIU	*adverb* more (quickly, softly, etc.)
PIX	less common spelling of *pyx*
PLU	*noun* (formerly in Canada) beaver skin used as a standard unit of value in the fur trade
PLY	*verb* work at (a job or trade); *noun* thickness of wool, fabric, etc.
POA	*noun* type of grass
POD	*noun* long narrow seed case of peas, beans, etc.; *verb* remove the pod from
POH	*interjection* exclamation expressing contempt or disgust; *verb* reject contemptuously
POI	*noun* ball of woven flax swung rhythmically by Māori women during special dances
POL	*noun* political campaigner
POM	*noun* Australian and New Zealand word for an English person
POO	*verb* a childish word for *defecate*
POP	*verb* make or cause to make a small explosive sound; *noun* small explosive sound; *adjective* popular

POS inflected form of *po*

POT *noun* round deep container; *verb* plant in a pot

POW *interjection* exclamation to indicate that a collision or explosion has taken place; *noun* head or a head of hair

POX *noun* disease in which skin pustules form; *verb* infect with pox

POZ *adjective* positive

PRE *preposition* before

PRO *preposition* in favour of; *noun* professional; *adverb* in favour of a motion etc.

PRY *verb* make an impertinent or uninvited inquiry into a private matter; *noun* act of prying

PSI *noun* twenty-third letter of the Greek alphabet

PST *interjection* sound made to attract someone's attention

PUB *noun* building with a bar licensed to sell alcoholic drinks; *verb* visit a pub or pubs

PUD short for *pudding*

PUG *noun* small snub-nosed dog; *verb* mix or knead (clay) with water to form a malleable mass or paste

PUH *interjection* exclamation expressing contempt or disgust

PUL *noun* Afghan monetary unit

PUN *noun* use of words to exploit double meanings for humorous effect; *verb* make puns

PUP *noun* young of certain animals, such as dogs and seals; *verb* (of dogs, seals, etc.) to give birth to pups

PUR same as *purr*

PUS *noun* yellowish matter produced by infected tissue

PUT *verb* cause to be (in a position, state, or place); *noun* throw in putting the shot

PUY *noun* small volcanic cone

PWN *verb* defeat (an opponent) in conclusive and humiliating fashion

PYA *noun* monetary unit of Myanmar worth one hundredth of a kyat

PYE same as *pie*

PYX *noun* any receptacle for the Eucharistic Host; *verb* put (something) in a pyx

QAT variant spelling of *kat*

QIN *noun* Chinese stringed instrument related to the zither

QIS inflected form of *qi*

QUA *preposition* in the capacity of

RAD *noun* former unit of absorbed ionizing radiation dose; *verb* fear; *adjective* slang term meaning great

RAG *noun* fragment of cloth; *verb* tease; *adjective* (in British universities and colleges) of various events organized to raise money for charity

RAH informal US word for *cheer*

RAI *noun* type of Algerian popular music

RAJ *noun* (in India) government

RAM *noun* male sheep; *verb* strike against with force

RAN inflected form of *run*

RAP *verb* hit with a sharp quick blow; *noun* quick sharp blow

RAS *noun* headland

RAT *noun* small rodent; *verb* inform (on)

RAV Hebrew word for *rabbi*

RAW *noun* as in *in the raw* without clothes; *adjective* uncooked

RAX *verb* stretch or extend; *noun* act of stretching or straining

RAY *noun* single line or narrow beam of light; *verb* (of an object) to emit (light) in rays or (of light) to issue in the form of rays

REB *noun* Confederate soldier in the American Civil War

REC short for *recreation*

RED *adjective* of a colour varying from crimson to orange and seen in blood, fire, etc.; *noun* red colour

REE *noun* Scots word meaning a walled enclosure

REF *noun* referee in sport; *verb* referee

REG *noun* large expanse of stony desert terrain

REH *noun* (in India) salty surface crust on the soil

REI *noun* name for a former Portuguese coin

REM *noun* dose of ionizing radiation

REN archaic variant of *run*

REO *noun* New Zealand language

REP *noun* sales representative; *verb* work as a representative

RES informal word for *residence*

RET *verb* moisten or soak (flax, hemp, jute, etc.) to facilitate separation of fibres

REV *noun* revolution (of an engine); *verb* increase the speed of revolution of (an engine)

REW archaic spelling of *rue*

REX *noun* king

REZ *noun* informal word for an instance of reserving; reservation

RHO *noun* seventeenth letter in the Greek alphabet

RHY archaic spelling of *rye*

RIA *noun* long narrow inlet of the seacoast

RIB *noun* one of the curved bones forming the framework of the upper part of the body; *verb* provide or mark with ribs

RID *verb* clear or relieve (of)

RIF *verb* lay off

RIG *verb* arrange in a dishonest way; *noun* apparatus for drilling for oil and gas

RIM *noun* edge or border; *verb* put a rim on (a pot, cup, wheel, etc.)

RIN Scots variant of *run*

RIP *verb* tear violently; *noun* split or tear

RIT *verb* Scots word meaning to cut or slit

RIZ (in some dialects) past form of *rise*

ROB *verb* steal from

ROC *noun* monstrous bird of Arabian mythology

ROD *noun* slender straight bar, stick; *verb* clear with a rod

ROE *noun* mass of eggs in a fish, sometimes eaten as food

ROK same as *roc*

ROM   *noun* male gypsy

ROO   *noun* kangaroo

ROT   *verb* decompose or decay; *noun* decay

ROW   *noun* straight line of people or things; *verb* propel (a boat) by oars

RUB   *verb* apply pressure with a circular or backwards-and-forwards movement; *noun* act of rubbing

RUC   same as *roc*

RUD   *noun* red or redness; *verb* redden

RUE   *verb* feel regret for; *noun* plant with evergreen bitter leaves

RUG   *noun* small carpet; *verb* (in dialect) tug

RUM   *noun* alcoholic drink distilled from sugar cane; *adjective* odd, strange

RUN   *verb* move with a more rapid gait than walking; *noun* act or spell of running

RUT   *noun* furrow made by wheels; *verb* be in a period of sexual excitability

RYA   *noun* type of rug originating in Scandinavia

RYE   *noun* kind of grain used for fodder and bread

RYU   *noun* school of Japanese martial arts

SAB   *noun* person engaged in direct action to prevent a targeted activity taking place; *verb* take part in such action

SAC *noun* pouchlike structure in an animal or plant

SAD *adjective* sorrowful, unhappy; *verb* New Zealand word meaning to express sadness or displeasure strongly

SAE Scots word for *so*

SAG *verb* sink in the middle; *noun* droop

SAI *noun* South American monkey

SAL pharmacological term for *salt*

SAM *verb* collect

SAN *noun* sanatorium

SAP *noun* moisture that circulates in plants; *verb* undermine

SAR *noun* marine fish; *verb* Scots word meaning to savour

SAT inflected form of *sit*

SAU archaic past tense of *see*

SAV *noun* saveloy: spicy smoked sausage

SAW *noun* hand tool for cutting wood and metal; *verb* cut with a saw

SAX same as *saxophone*

SAY *verb* speak or utter; *noun* right or chance to speak

SAZ *noun* Middle Eastern stringed instrument

SEA *noun* mass of salt water covering three quarters

of the earth's surface

SEC *noun* secant: (in trigonometry) the ratio of the length of the hypotenuse to the length of the adjacent side

SED old spelling of *said*

SEE *verb* perceive with the eyes or mind; *noun* diocese of a bishop

SEG *noun* metal stud on shoe sole

SEI *noun* type of rorqual: the largest group of baleen whales

SEL Scots word for *self*

SEN *noun* monetary unit of Brunei, Cambodia, Indonesia, Malaysia, and formerly of Japan

SER *noun* unit of weight used in India

SET *verb* put in a specified position or state; *noun* setting or being set; *adjective* fixed or established beforehand

SEV *noun* Indian snack of deep-fried noodles

SEW *verb* join with thread repeatedly passed through with a needle

SEX *noun* state of being male or female; *verb* find out the sex of; *adjective* of sexual matters

SEY *noun* Scots word meaning part of cow carcass

SEZ *verb* informal spelling of *says*

SHA *interjection* be quiet

SHE *pronoun* female person or animal previously mentioned; *noun* female person or animal

SHH *interjection* sound made to ask for silence

SHO *adjective* sure, as pronounced in southern US

SHY *adjective* not at ease in company; *verb* start back in fear; *noun* throw

SIB *noun* blood relative

SIC *adverb* thus; *verb* attack

SIF *adjective* (South African slang) disgusting

SIG short for *signature*

SIK *adjective* excellent

SIM *noun* computer game that simulates an activity

SIN *noun* offence or transgression; *verb* commit a sin

SIP *verb* drink in small mouthfuls; *noun* amount sipped

SIR *noun* polite term of address for a man; *verb* call someone 'sir'

SIS *noun* sister

SIT *verb* rest one's body upright on the buttocks

SIX *noun* one more than five

SKA *noun* type of pop music from the Caribbean

SKI *noun* one of a pair of long runners fastened to boots for gliding over snow or water; *verb* travel on skis

SKY *noun* upper atmosphere as seen from the earth; *verb* hit high in the air

SLY *adjective* crafty

SMA Scots word for *small*

SNY *noun* side channel of a river

SOB *verb* weep with convulsive gasps; *noun* act or sound of sobbing

SOC *noun* feudal right to hold court

SOD *noun* (piece of) turf; *verb* cover with sods

SOG *verb* soak

SOH *noun* (in tonic sol-fa) fifth degree of any major scale

SOL *noun* liquid colloidal solution

SOM *noun* currency of Kyrgyzstan and Uzbekistan

SON *noun* male offspring

SOP *noun* concession to pacify someone; *verb* mop up or absorb (liquid)

SOS inflected form of *so*

SOT *noun* habitual drunkard; *adverb* indeed: used to contradict a negative statement; *verb* be a drunkard

SOU *noun* former French coin

SOV shortening of *sovereign*

SOW *verb* scatter or plant (seed) in or on (the ground); *noun* female adult pig

SOX informal spelling of *socks*

SOY *noun* as in *soy sauce* salty dark brown sauce made from soya beans

SOZ *interjection* (slang) sorry

SPA *noun* resort with a mineral-water spring; *verb* visit a spa

SPY *noun* person employed to obtain secret information; *verb* act as a spy

SRI *noun* title of respect used when addressing a Hindu

STY *verb* climb

SUB *noun* subeditor; *verb* act as a substitute

SUD singular of *suds*

SUE *verb* start legal proceedings against

SUG *verb* sell a product while pretending to conduct market research

SUI *adjective* of itself

SUK *noun* souk: open-air marketplace

SUM *noun* result of addition, total; *verb* add or form a total of (something)

SUN *noun* star around which the earth and other planets revolve; *verb* expose (oneself) to the sun's rays

SUP *verb* have supper

SUQ same as *suk*

SUR *preposition* above

SUS suss: *verb* attempt to work out (a situation, etc.), using one's intuition; *noun* sharpness of mind

SWY *noun* Australian gambling game involving two coins

SYE *verb* strain

SYN Scots word for *since*

TAB *noun* small flap or projecting label; *verb* supply with a tab

TAD *noun* small bit or piece

TAE *preposition* Scots form of to; *verb* Scots form of toe

TAG *noun* label bearing information; *verb* attach a tag to

TAI *noun* type of sea bream

TAJ *noun* tall conical cap worn as a mark of distinction by Muslims

TAK Scots variant spelling of *take*

TAM *noun* type of hat

TAN *noun* brown coloration of the skin from exposure to sunlight; *verb* (of skin) go brown from exposure to sunlight; *adjective* yellowish-brown

TAO *noun* (in Confucian philosophy) the correct course of action

TAP *verb* knock lightly and usually repeatedly; *noun* light knock

TAR *noun* thick black liquid distilled from coal etc.; *verb* coat with tar

TAS tass: *noun* cup, goblet, or glass

TAT *noun* tatty or tasteless article(s); *verb* make a type of lace by looping a thread with a hand shuttle

TAU *noun* nineteenth letter in the Greek alphabet

TAV *noun* twenty-third and last letter in the Hebrew alphabet

TAW *verb* convert skins into leather

TAX *noun* compulsory payment levied by a government on income, property, etc. to raise revenue; *verb* levy a tax on

TAY Irish dialect word for *tea*

TEA *noun* drink made from infusing the dried leaves of an Asian bush in boiling water; *verb* take tea

TEC short for *detective*

TED	*verb* shake out (hay), so as to dry it
TEE	*noun* small peg from which a golf ball can be played at the start of each hole; *verb* position (the ball) ready for striking, on or as if on a tee
TEF	*noun* annual grass, of North East Africa, grown for its grain
TEG	*noun* two-year-old sheep
TEL	same as *tell*
TEN	*noun* one more than nine; *adjective* amounting to ten
TES	inflected form of *te*
TET	*noun* ninth letter of the Hebrew alphabet
TEW	*verb* work hard
TEX	*noun* unit of weight used to measure yarn density
THE	*determiner* definite article, used before a noun
THO	short for *though*
THY	*adjective* of or associated with you (thou); *determiner* belonging to or associated in some way with you (thou)
TIC	*noun* spasmodic muscular twitch
TID	*noun* girl

TIE   *verb* fasten or be fastened with string, rope, etc.; *noun* long narrow piece of material worn knotted round the neck

TIG   *noun* child's game

TIK   *noun* South African slang word for methamphetamine

TIL   another name for *sesame*

TIN   *noun* soft metallic element; *verb* put (food) into tins

TIP   *noun* narrow or pointed end of anything; *verb* put a tip on

TIS   inflected form of *ti*

TIT   *noun* any of various small songbirds; *verb* jerk or tug

TIX   *plural noun* tickets

TIZ   *noun* state of confusion

TOC   *noun* in communications code, signal for letter T

TOD   *noun* unit of weight, used for wool, etc.; *verb* produce a tod

TOE   *noun* digit of the foot; *verb* touch or kick with the toe

TOG   *noun* unit for measuring the insulating power of duvets; *verb* dress oneself

TOM   *noun* male cat; *adjective* (of an animal) male

TON   *noun* unit of weight

TOO   *adverb* also, as well

TOP   *noun* highest point or part; *adjective* at or of the top; *verb* form a top on

TOR   *noun* high rocky hill

TOT   *noun* small child; *verb* total

TOW   *verb* drag, esp by means of a rope; *noun* towing

TOY   *noun* something designed to be played with; *adjective* designed to be played with; *verb* play, fiddle, or flirt

TRY   *verb* make an effort or attempt; *noun* attempt or effort

TSK   *verb* utter the sound 'tsk', usually in disapproval

TUB   *noun* open, usually round container; *verb* wash (oneself or another) in a tub

TUG   *verb* pull hard; *noun* hard pull

TUI   *noun* New Zealand honeyeater that mimics human speech and the songs of other birds

TUM   informal or childish word for *stomach*

TUN   *noun* large beer cask; *verb* put into or keep in tuns

TUP   *noun* male sheep; *verb* cause (a ram) to mate with a ewe

TUT	*interjection* exclamation of mild disapproval, or surprise; *verb* express disapproval by the exclamation of 'tut-tut'; *noun* payment system based on measurable work done
TUX	*noun* tuxedo: dinner jacket
TWA	Scots word for *two*
TWO	*noun* one more than one
TWP	*adjective* stupid
TYE	*noun* trough used in mining to separate valuable material from dross; *verb* (in mining) isolate valuable material from dross using a tye
TYG	*noun* mug with two handles
UDO	*noun* stout perennial plant of Japan and China
UDS	*interjection* God
UEY	*noun* u-turn
UFO	*noun* flying saucer
UGH	*interjection* exclamation of disgust; *noun* sound made to indicate disgust
UGS	inflected form of *ug*
UKE	short form of *ukulele*
ULE	*noun* rubber tree
ULU	*noun* type of knife
UME	*noun* sour Japanese fruit
UMM	same as *um*

UMP	umpire: *noun* official who rules on the playing of a game; *verb* act as umpire in (a game)
UMS	inflected form of *um*
UMU	*noun* type of oven
UNI	*noun* university
UNS	inflected form of *un*
UPO	*preposition* upon
UPS	inflected form of *up*
URB	*noun* urban area
URD	*noun* type of plant with edible seeds
URE	*noun* extinct European wild ox
URN	*noun* vase used as a container for the ashes of the dead; *verb* put in an urn
URP	dialect word for *vomit*
USE	*verb* put into service or action; *noun* using or being used
UTA	*noun* side-blotched lizard
UTE	same as *utility*
UTS	inflected form of *ut*
UTU	*noun* reward
UVA	*noun* grape or fruit resembling this
VAC	*verb* clean with a vacuum cleaner
VAE	same as *voe*

VAG   *noun* vagrant

VAN   *noun* motor vehicle for transporting goods; *verb* send in a van

VAR   *noun* unit of reactive power of an alternating current

VAS   *noun* vessel or tube that carries a fluid

VAT   *noun* large container for liquids; *verb* place, store, or treat in a vat

VAU   same as *vav*

VAV   *noun* sixth letter of the Hebrew alphabet

VAW   *noun* Hebrew letter

VAX   *noun* vaccination

VEE   *noun* letter V

VEG   *noun* vegetable or vegetables; *verb* relax

VET   *verb* check the suitability of; *noun* military veteran

VEX   *verb* frustrate, annoy

VIA   *preposition* by way of; *noun* road

VID   same as *video*

VIE   *verb* compete (with someone)

VIG   *noun* interest on a loan that is paid to a moneylender

VIM   *noun* force, energy

VIN   *noun* French wine

VIS	*noun* power, force, or strength
VLY	*noun* area of low marshy ground
VOE	*noun* (in Orkney and Shetland) a small bay or narrow creek
VOG	*noun* air pollution caused by volcanic dust
VOL	*noun* heraldic wings
VOM	*verb* vomit
VOR	*verb* (in dialect) warn
VOW	*noun* solemn and binding promise; *verb* promise solemnly
VOX	*noun* voice or sound
VUG	*noun* small cavity in a rock or vein, usually lined with crystals
VUM	*verb* swear
WAB	*noun* web
WAD	*noun* black earthy ore of manganese; *noun* small mass of soft material; *verb* form (something) into a wad
WAE	old form of *woe*
WAG	*verb* move rapidly from side to side; *noun* wagging movement
WAI	*noun* (in New Zealand) water
WAN	*adjective* pale and sickly looking; *verb* make or become wan

WAP *verb* strike

WAR *noun* fighting between nations; *adjective* of, like, or caused by war; *verb* conduct a war

WAS past tense of *be*

WAT *adjective* wet; drunken

WAW another name for *vav*

WAX *noun* solid shiny fatty or oily substance used for sealing, making candles, etc.; *verb* coat or polish with wax

WAY *noun* manner or method; *verb* travel

WAZ *verb* urinate; *noun* act of urinating

WEB *noun* net spun by a spider; *verb* cover with or as if with a web

WED *verb* marry

WEE *adjective* small or short; *noun* instance of urinating; *verb* urinate

WEM *noun* belly, abdomen, or womb

WEN *noun* cyst on the scalp

WET *adjective* covered or soaked with water or another liquid; *noun* moisture or rain; *verb* make wet

WEX obsolete form of *wax*

WEY *noun* measurement of weight

WHA Scots word for *who*

WHO *pronoun* which person

WHY *adverb* for what reason; *pronoun* because of which; *noun* reason, purpose, or cause of something

WIG *noun* artificial head of hair; *verb* furnish with a wig

WIN *verb* come first in (a competition, fight, etc.); *noun* victory, esp in a game

WIS *verb* know or suppose (something)

WIT *verb* detect; *noun* ability to use words or ideas in a clever and amusing way

WIZ shortened form of *wizard*

WOE *noun* grief

WOF *noun* fool

WOK *noun* bowl-shaped Chinese cooking pan, used for stir-frying

WON *noun* monetary unit of North Korea; *verb* live or dwell

WOO *verb* seek the love or affection of someone

WOP *verb* strike, beat, or thrash; *noun* heavy blow or the sound made by such a blow

WOS inflected form of *wo*

WOT past tense of *wit*

WOW *interjection* exclamation of astonishment; *noun* astonishing person or thing; *verb* be a great success with

WOX past tense of *wax*

WRY *adjective* drily humorous; *verb* twist or contort

WUD Scots form of *wood*

WUS *noun* casual term of address

WUZ *verb* nonstandard spelling of *was*

WYE *noun* y-shaped pipe

WYN *noun* rune equivalent to English *w*

XED *verb* marked a cross against

XIS inflected form of *xi*

YAD *noun* hand-held pointer used for reading the sefer torah

YAE same as *ae*

YAG *noun* artificial crystal

YAH *interjection* exclamation of derision or disgust; *noun* affected upper-class person

YAK *noun* Tibetan ox with long shaggy hair; *verb* talk continuously about unimportant matters

YAM *noun* tropical root vegetable

YAP *verb* bark with a high-pitched sound; *noun* high-pitched bark

YAR *adjective* nimble

YAS inflected form of *ya*

YAW *verb* (of an aircraft or ship) turn to one side or from side to side while moving; *noun* act or movement of yawing

YAY	*noun* cry of approval
YEA	*interjection* yes; *adverb* indeed or truly; *sentence substitute* aye; *noun* cry of agreement
YEH	*noun* positive affirmation
YEN	*noun* monetary unit of Japan; *verb* have a longing
YEP	*noun* affirmative statement
YER	*adjective* (colloquial) your; you
YES	*interjection* expresses consent, agreement, or approval; *noun* answer or vote of yes, used to express acknowledgment, affirmation, consent, etc.; *verb* reply in the affirmative
YET	*adverb* up until then or now
YEW	*noun* evergreen tree with needle-like leaves and red berries
YEX	*verb* hiccup
YEZ	*interjection* yes
YGO	archaic past participle of *go*
YIN	Scots word for *one*
YIP	*verb* emit a high-pitched bark
YOB	*noun* bad-mannered aggressive youth
YOD	*noun* tenth letter in the Hebrew alphabet
YOK	*verb* chuckle

YOM *noun* day

YON *adjective* that or those over there; *adverb* yonder; *pronoun* that person or thing

YOU *pronoun* person or people addressed; *noun* personality of the person being addressed

YOW *verb* howl

YUG *noun* (in Hindu cosmology) one of the four ages of mankind

YUK *interjection* exclamation indicating contempt, dislike, or disgust; *verb* chuckle

YUM *interjection* expressing delight

YUP *noun* informal affirmative statement

YUS inflected form of *yu*

ZAG *verb* change direction sharply

ZAP *verb* kill (by shooting); *noun* energy, vigour, or pep; *interjection* exclamation used to express sudden or swift action

ZAS inflected form of *za*

ZAX *noun* tool for cutting roofing slate

ZEA *noun* corn silk

ZED *noun* British and New Zealand spoken form of the letter Z

ZEE the US word for *zed*

ZEK *noun* Soviet prisoner

ZEL *noun* Turkish cymbal

ZEN	*noun* calm meditative state
ZEP	*noun* type of long sandwich
ZEX	*noun* tool for cutting roofing slate
ZHO	same as *zo*
ZIG	same as *zag*
ZIN	*noun* zinfandel: type of Californian wine
ZIP	same as *zipper*
ZIT	*noun* spot or pimple
ZIZ	*noun* short sleep; *verb* take a short sleep, snooze
ZOA	plural of *zoon* (independent animal body)
ZOL	*noun* (South African slang) a cannabis cigarette
ZOO	*noun* place where live animals are kept for show
ZOS	inflected form of *zo*
ZUZ	*noun* ancient Hebrew silver coin
ZZZ	informal word for *sleep*

Essential Scrabble Glossary

Blockers are words which cannot have a letter added to either the beginning or the end. This means blockers often 'close down' part of the board.

Bonuses are words, usually seven or eight letters long, which use all of your tiles to give you an extra 50 points.

Floaters are letters that are available on the board for you to use as part of another word, and to play onto.

Hooks are letters that transform an existing word into another valid word when adding them at the beginning or the end. For example:

EARFUL can take a T at the front to make TEARFUL

SOD can take an A at the end to make SODA

Worth a Play, Read and Watch

Word Freak – Heartbreak, Triumph, Genius and Obsession in the World of Competitive Scrabble Players is a best-selling book by Wall Street journalist Stefan Fatsis. It tells of an ordinary guy starting out in the 'Scrabble World' and is a really excellent read.

Word Wars – Tiles and Tribulations on the Scrabble Game Circuit is a funny real-life documentary by Eric Chaikin, focusing on four top US Scrabblers.

Collins Official Scrabble Words contains the full list of words allowed in Scrabble, without meanings, while *Collins Scrabble Dictionary* includes brief definitions for words from two to nine letters in length.

If you prefer full definitions, there's always *Collins English Dictionary* to while away the time.

For a bit of variety, *Bananagrams®*, *Boggle*, Channel 4's *Countdown* and *Scrabble Trickster* are all good Scrabble practice.

Top UK player David Webb plays two games every week featuring live commentary. He has also put together a series of excellent short video blogs, summing up the highlights of recent major tournaments. They can be found on the *Dweebovision* Channel on YouTube.

Taking It Further

There are over 300 Scrabble clubs in the UK, normally meeting weekly with an average membership of fifteen. Two or three games are played over an evening in a variety of venues ranging from homes to pubs to village halls, and there are competitions, leagues and trophies to be won over a season.

Joining a club is the first step towards Scrabble seriousness and can be quite daunting to start with. Just remember the vast majority of club players are extremely pleasant and don't be put off by the over-competitive minority.

There is a Scrabble event to be found somewhere in the UK on almost every weekend of the year.

The numbers of players can range from ten to a hundred, and the larger tournaments contain more than one division, so you're placed with players of a similar standard. There are usually six or seven games in a one-day event – weekends can take in around sixteen.

If you don't take it too seriously they can be great fun. The only big difference from playing at home or at a club is the use of timers to ensure the games last under an hour and no one holds up the schedule – they don't take long to get used to operating.

The ABSP is the Association of British Scrabble Players and is effectively the game's governing body.

It costs £25 a year to join (there are about 600 members), and for that you get an excellent bi-monthly newsletter and various tournament discounts (membership is only £12.50 if you get the newsletter online). The ABSP website can be found at **www.absp.org.uk** and contains everything you need to know about what's going on in 'UK Scrabble'. There's a tournament calendar, event results, rankings and word lists and plenty of other useful material for the aspiring player.

If you are interested in joining a Scrabble club, you can get all the information you need by visiting **www.absp.org.uk/play**

There are also some very exciting initiatives such as:

1) Tablet Scrabble
A joint venture from 2017 UK National Champion Austin Shin – the only UK player ever to win the US Championship – and 2017 World Champion David Eldar from Australia. It would be hard to find a better twosome than that. The idea is to play Scrabble on tablets rather than boards to get the massive throngs of online players, particularly students, interested in playing competitive Scrabble.

2) Prison Scrabble

This is my 'baby' – the idea being to set up Prison Scrabble Clubs to help educate prisoners in literacy and numeracy and simultaneously keep them busy. Watch this space…

3) Schools Scrabble

Scrabble is now officially in the School Curriculum in Thailand and Nigeria. Many of the top Nigerian Scrabblers are actually now employed as coaches around the country.

4) International Scrabble

Whereas a decade or so ago there were only three or four international tournaments on the Scrabble calendar, you can now find one somewhere in the world pretty much every weekend. WESPA – World English-language Scrabble Players Association – are the governing body, see **www.wespa.org.**

There is a huge online Scrabble presence – with ISC you can play anyone around the world in real time and you get your own rating. 'Scrabble GO' is a snappy version including lots of other word games, such as six moves/game duels. They are both free resources. There are also excellent websites *Scrabble Snippetz* and *Scrabble International*.

The future of Scrabble, in the safe hands of some amazing players, is very very bright.

Collins
LITTLE BOOKS

These beautifully presented Little Books make excellent pocket-sized guides, packed with hints and tips.

101 Ways to Win at Scrabble	978-0-00-758914-2	£6.99
Bananagrams® Secrets	978-0-00-825046-1	£6.99
Bridge Secrets	978-0-00-825047-8	£6.99
Card Games	978-0-00-830653-3	£6.99
Clans and Tartans	978-0-00-825109-3	£6.99
Craft Beer	978-0-00-827120-6	£6.99
English Castles	978-0-00-829833-3	£6.99
English Cathedrals	978-0-00-829832-6	£6.99
English History	978-0-00-829813-5	£6.99
Irish Castles	978-0-00-834822-9	£6.99
Irish History	978-0-00-834013-1	£6.99
Irish Whiskey	978-0-00-834066-7	£6.99
Gin	978-0-00-825810-8	£6.99
Rum	978-0-00-827122-0	£6.99
Scots Dictionary	978-0-00-828552-4	£6.99
Scottish Castles	978-0-00-825111-6	£6.99
Scottish Dance	978-0-00-821056-4	£6.99
Scottish History	978-0-00-825110-9	£6.99
Whisky	978-0-00-825108-6	£6.99

Available to buy from all good booksellers and online.
All titles are also available as ebooks.
www.collins.co.uk

 @collins_ref    facebook.com/collinsref